GOD and SCIENCE
The Death and Rebirth of Theism

Charles P. Henderson, Jr.

John Knox Press
ATLANTA

Library of Congress Cataloging-in-Publication Data

Henderson, Charles P.
   God and science.

   Bibliography: p.
   Includes index.
   1. Religion and science—1946–   . 2. Atheism.
3. Theism.   I. Title.
BL240.2.H38   1986   231   85-23091
ISBN 0-8042-0668-6

© copyright John Knox Press 1986
10 9 8 7 6 5 4 3 2 1
Printed in the United States of America
John Knox Press
Atlanta, Georgia 30365

Acknowledgment is made for permission to quote from the following sources:

To The Christian Century Foundation for material in altered form from Charles P. Henderson, Jr., "Theology for a Secular Age," *The Christian Century* (January 1980), copyright © 1980 by The Christian Century Foundation. Reprinted by permission.

To Doubleday for excerpts from DOES GOD EXIST? by Hans Küng, copyright © 1978, 1979, 1980 by Doubleday & Company, Inc. Reprinted by permission of the publisher.

To Harcourt Brace Jovanovich, Inc. for excerpts from "How I Believe" in CHRISTIANITY AND EVOLUTION by Pierre Teilhard de Chardin, copyright © 1969 by Editions du Seuil; English translation copyright © 1969 by William Collins Sons & Co. Ltd. Reprinted by permission of Harcourt Brace Jovanovich, Inc. For Figure 2, "'Modern' Type of Cosmogenesis," p. 194 from CHRISTIANITY AND EVOLUTION by Pierre Teilhard de Chardin, copyright © 1969 by Editions du Seuil, English translation copyright © 1971 by William Collins Sons & Co. Ltd. and Harcourt Brace Jovanovich, Inc. Reprinted by permission of Harcourt Brace Jovanovich, Inc. For excerpt from HUMAN ENERGY by Pierre Teilhard de Chardin, copyright © 1962 by Editions du Seuil; English translation copyright © 1969 by William Collins Ltd. Reprinted by permission of Harcourt Brace Jovanovich, Inc.

To Harper & Row, Publishers, Inc. for excerpts from Pierre Teilhard de Chardin, *The Divine Milieu*, © copyright 1969; Pierre Teilhard de Chardin, *The Future of Man*, © copyright 1969; Pierre Teilhard de Chardin, *The Phenomenon of Man*, © copyright 1961; and Werner Heisenberg, *Physics and Beyond*, © copyright 1971. Reprinted by permission of Harper & Row, Publishers, Inc.

To Shambhala Publication, Inc. for excerpts from THE TAO OF PHYSICS by Fritjof Capra, © 1975. Reprinted with permission from Shambhala Publications, Boston, MA.

To Viking Penguin Inc. for excerpts from THE PORTABLE KARL MARX, edited by Eugene Kamenka. Copyright © 1983 by Viking Penguin Inc. All Rights Reserved. Reprinted by permission of Viking Penguin Inc.

To William Morrow & Company, Inc. for about 1,500 words abridged from THE DANCING WU LI MASTERS by Gary Zukav. Copyright © 1979 by Gary Zukav. By permission of William Morrow & Company.

To W. W. Norton & Company. The lines from *The Future of an Illusion* by Sigmund Freud, translated by James Strachey, are used by permission of W. W. Norton & Company, Inc. Copyright © 1961 by James Strachey.

Acknowledgments

I would like to express my gratitude to friends and colleagues who helped me summon the time, energy, and imagination necessary in the writing of this book. Thanks to Bruce Smith for running the entire manuscript through his word processor; thanks to my colleagues at Central Church, especially Katharine Hoffman and Pat Guss; appreciation also to the many critics and respondents in the congregation, especially Chet Burger and Nancy Smith; and for similar contributions from Jim McCord, Lee Hancock, Nancy Becker, Barbara Wheeler, and James Murphy. In Vermont, much valuable logistical support was provided by my friends and neighbors, John and Diana Price. Jim Wall at *The Christian Century* and John Gibbs at John Knox Press each had a hand in getting this book into print. Behind and before all these stand the many gifted teachers at Union and Auburn Theological Seminaries in New York City and, of course, my family, through which some currents in this book can be traced back to the third and fourth generations.

Charles P. Henderson, Jr.
New York, New York

Contents

Introduction

 This book was conceived and written in New York City and Athens, Vermont. In New York, where I serve as minister of Central Presbyterian Church, I am constantly aware of how profoundly this civilization is shaped by science and technology. As I walk the streets and avenues of this great city, it often strikes me that I am not treading upon mother earth; rather, I am traversing a maze of concrete and steel. In New York one walks over a labyrinth of wires and pipes—telephone wires and sewage pipes, power lines and steam conveying pipes. Beneath all this plumbing and electrical equipment, there is the vault of the subway system. In New York we are surrounded on all sides by the products of human inventiveness: giant buildings soaring upwards, jet aircraft circling overhead in intricate patterns, satellites in orbit around the earth itself. Here we live in a cocoon of science and technology.

Traveling north toward Vermont one gradually peels away layer after layer from this crust of civilization. Cities are replaced by towns and towns by villages, and gradually the fields and mountains prevail. On the hillside where I sit down to write I am surrounded by trees and flowers; my writing companions are field mice and a beautiful pair of cedar waxwings, creatures of yellow and black, brown and gray that feed upon the mulberries and blueberries growing in front of my cabin. Here it is possible to enter into a direct relationship with the land, with clouds and sun, with nature, and with nature's God. In Vermont, I am aware there is an infinite, qualitative difference between living in a world which is generally believed to be the direct creation of God and living in a culture shaped by human hands, and it is the city which prefigures the future. Even in Vermont the forests are invaded by snowmobiles and chain saws, and acid rain slowly wrecks havoc among the trees. More importantly, even in this remote location people have come to see the world through the lens of science, and technology provides the tools and instruments which are mediators in our relationship to the natural world. Here television and radio interpret changes in the weather to be the result of shifts in the direction of the jet stream, cold fronts, or high pressure zones which trace their path across the surface of our planet. Photographs of the weather maps are received directly from satellites through a giant disk antenna located in a neighbor's wheat field. It sits here in eloquent testimony to the all-persuasive presence of technology.

In this civilization of science and technology it is no longer necessary to label every natural phenomenon as an act of God. In fact, just the opposite is true. We tend to consider every other explanation for the significant events of life. Wars are the result of geopolitical conflicts among nations and empires; crime rates reflect underlying societal pressures; the rate of unemployment is tied to policies of giant bureaucracies; the innermost feelings of the individual are understood in scientific perspective as events in the chemical and electrical circuitry of the brain. Increasingly we see our lives as being shaped by forces that are entirely within the sphere of science.

Rather than seeing God as the Lord and Sovereign of all, we have come to view ourselves as the arbiters of our own fate. For many people this new view of the world brings with it a sense of freedom and liberation. There is a sense of exhilaration in the discovery that we are responsible for our own future. Yet with our new freedom we are also forced to bear the burden of human choice. In a scientific and technical age almost everything has to be decided from scratch. We are presented with a choice of fashions and a choice of foods, a choice of life-styles and even a choice of religions. Rather than standing in awe before nature, we stand bewildered by the magnitude and complexity of our own decisions.

Science and technology have given us the power to change and mold the environment itself, to interfere in the process of human reproduction, to create life in a test tube, even to invent new life forms if that is our will. We have the power to create and we also have the power to destroy. Our atomic weapons have given us the power to render the earth uninhabitable if that is our decision. How little we understand about the new forces which science and technology have unleashed upon the world.

Whether one contemplates the awesome proliferation of nuclear weapons or the persistent problems in our schools and colleges, whether one looks at the world situation at large or the confusion and disorder in our personal lives, it is apparent that we have not achieved mastery over the very systems we have created. The culture of technology is in some ways as confusing, as bewildering, and as awesome as the world of untrammeled nature, and we no longer have the solace of saying, by way of explanation, that current events are the direct result of divine intervention.

All this is devastating to the foundations of traditional religion. For it is and always has been the unique claim of biblical faith that God is the Alpha and the Omega, the Beginning and the End, the One in whom all things cohere. On the surface at least it would seem that this is a most unlikely time for such a claim to be put forward with persuasiveness. In this age of science and specialization reality itself seems to be divided into several distinct categories. Like the sections of a news magazine, our consciousness is carved up into separate subheadings: news of the world, the arts, fashion and sports, science, and then, of course, religion which itself is divided according to denomination, sect, and type. In fact the *New York Times* has an editor to cover religious news, and *Time* magazine reports religion in a brief section at the "back of the book." It is perfectly in keeping with a culture of pluralism, but this accommodation to diversity reveals a crisis of fundamental importance for the Judeo-Christian tradition. A God who can be relegated to the back of a book or seen as belonging to the periphery of consciousness is not the God of the Bible. Today God suffers not so much from direct attack by atheists or agnostics but from the willingness on the part of the most devout believers to allow reality itself to be compartmentalized into entirely independent realms. A God whose rule is limited to the private realm of religious experience has already been reduced to a position of impotence. With God so marginalized is it any wonder that a sense of spiritual malaise looms over the whole of western culture?

As almost everyone from the President to a ward politician would affirm, we face a spiritual crisis, but the severity of the crisis is not to be measured in statistics on church attendance, changes in conventional morality, or opinion polls measuring the popularity of God. The problem is basically a failure of religious imagination. The present situation requires a new way of thinking about God commensurate to the challenge presented by a culture of science and technology.

Perhaps the greatest single obstacle to this task of reconstruction is the widely perceived conflict between science and religion. For several generations of Americans, the ideas and intellectual movements associated with science have been seen to be antithetical to faith. At the same time, the impression has been created that religion is fighting a rearguard action against the advancing armies of human knowledge. As we learn more and more about the great mysteries of life, there seems to be less and less justification for belief in God. Whole generations of college students in the period since World War II have been introduced to the idea that God is merely an intellectual crutch. God belongs to the old world of myth and superstition, soon to be replaced by the new world of high technology. Of course, God still scores high in the opinion polls, but for many of the college graduates who have now become the shapers of secular culture God is seen as a philosophical dinosaur whose time of extinction is near. God's only remaining purpose is to fill the remaining gaps in human knowledge and answer the yet unanswered questions.

This situation has been exacerbated by religious leaders who have taken a defensive posture in the face of the new science. The very idea that all truth claims must be challenged and tested through a process of rational inquiry has been seen as a threat to the authority of the Bible and the church alike. In other words, the fundamental approach to knowledge which we call the scientific method is felt to have a corrosive effect upon religious doctrine and tradition.

Tragically this defensive attitude in the face of modern science is evident in the work of the world's greatest theologians, not just those who insist on the literal inerrancy of the Scriptures. For example, religious leaders of no less importance than Dietrich Bonhoeffer have surrendered practically the whole domain of human knowledge to a God-less science:

> Man has learnt to deal with himself in all questions of importance without recourse to the "working hypothesis" called "God." In questions of science, art, and ethics this has become an understood thing at which one now hardly dares to tilt. But for the last hundred years or so it has also become increasingly true of religious questions; it is becoming evident that everything gets along without "God"—and, in fact, just as well as before. As in the scientific field, so in human affairs generally, "God" is being pushed more and more out of life, losing more and more ground.[1]

Accordingly, many theologians have retreated from the task of entering into dialogue with the secular world, and both science and religion are left to pursue their private interests, largely in a state of isolation. This situation is tragic for both the scientists and the theologians, and it is doubly tragic for western culture as a whole. For, if God can no longer be seen as the organizing principle of reality, then our whole world view, our value system, and even consciousness itself are split right down the middle. Fortunately there is now reason to believe that this impasse between the secular and the sacred is not a permanent condition. This book is written in the conviction that the stalemate between science and religion can be broken and our situation of conflict can be resolved, if scientists and religious leaders alike become aware of the similar crosscurrents in their respective domains.

There are several developments in the culture of technology which set the stage for a rapprochement with religion. Reflect, for example, upon the implications of a global system of communications and worldwide energy crisis which heighten public awareness of the interdependence of widely separate peoples. Consider the scientific findings which expose the mystery, unpredictability, even the lawless character of the natural world. Ponder the implications of a depth psychology which emphasizes the irrational and the role of the unconscious in human behavior. Take account of those political theories which emphasize the interconnecting structures operative in the political and economic sphere. It is surprising how many of these apparently unrelated phenomena are consistent with a view of the world which arises from the monotheism of the Bible.

In a world where all the contestants for ultimate allegiance suffer from a lack of credibility, monotheistic religion can do its work of exposing the false idols and icons of culture with greater success than ever before. In a world where interdependence is seen not only as a fact of life but also as the basis for a new ethic, a biblical faith raises the question of depth. At what level and in what dimension of depth does interdependence become normative? In a world where scientific research makes it increasingly clear how much mystery and paradox there appears to be at the heart of all things, monotheism can continue to define the mystery as a manifestation of the holy. In a world increasingly aware of the complexities, hidden depths, and tragic cross-purposes of the human personality, the Judeo-Christian tradition can point to the possibility for redemption; that is, for the unification of consciousness under the rule of a just and loving God. In a world where all religious experience is held up to a critical analysis and attack, monotheism can continue its work of exposing the element of faith which is hidden within every doubt. Above all, advocates of a biblical faith can point to the divine presence which is above and beyond every flawed conception of God.

In what follows I will attempt to show that there is no better way to begin one's search for a deeper faith than at the doors of doubt. The major criticisms of religion which have been put forward in the past two hundred years, largely in the name and under the banner of modern science, must be taken with utmost seriousness. One must pursue all the reasonable arguments of contemporary atheism, for behind them all may be found the resources for the building of a greater and deeper faith. When one pursues the precise logic of skepticism, one discovers nothing less than a new case for theism. When one carries the new scientific theories to their logical conclusions, more often than not, one discovers surprising confirmation for the most ancient insights of religion. In fact, all the arguments that are used today in defiance of God may be turned inside out to be used in God's defense.

This book takes the reader on an intellectual pilgrimage through doubt to faith, through science to religion, through the unrelenting rigor of skepticism to the threshold of what may be a profound religious awakening. I will look in some depth at the questions raised by the major scientific movements of the modern period. I will examine critically the challenges to religion that have been put forward in the names of Einstein and Freud, Darwin and Marx. I will examine those illusory boundary lines separating science and religion, sexuality and spirituality, church and state in order to discover, at those very points where God has been felt to be most problematic, new insights and signals of God's presence.

If God is truly the Alpha and the Omega, the Beginning and the End, the One in whom all things cohere, then it should be evident that the apparently separate realms of our personal and public life, our politics and our organized religions, our arts and sciences, are in fact fused together under the rule of God. This book is conceived in the belief that the monotheism of the Bible, mediated and interpreted in the light of modern science, may be the only effective means we have of binding together the broken pieces of our lives and moving forward with a renewed sense of purpose and grace.

In the course of making this case I circle back in time, first to the opening decades of the twentieth century where the crosscurrents of science and religion meet in the work of Albert Einstein and Sigmund Freud. Finding, especially in Freud, that religion and science appear to be in a state of opposition, I trace the roots of this conflict back to the work of Darwin and Marx.

In their writing we see the gathering force of what I have called "scientific atheism." In their work and in reaction to it, the argument is made with greater and greater force that in order for science to be thoroughly scientific it must be thoroughly separated from religion. At the same time, we observe religion in a steady state of retreat. Though the nineteenth century opened with leading theologians firmly convinced that science provided strong support for faith and that one could construct stronger and stronger arguments for God, the century closed with science and religion practically at war with each other. Meanwhile, the very effort to prove the existence of God was abandoned by the theologians themselves.

Working forward toward the present, I examine the works of two theologians who tried valiantly to break the stalemate between science and theology, namely, Pierre Teilhard de Chardin and Paul Tillich. Fighting in many ways against the mainstream of theology in the first half of the twentieth century, these two men succeeded in setting the stage for reconciliation of the scientific and the theological. They also laid the foundations for a new case for theism. In chapter 7 I examine the work of two writers who exhibit the extreme paralysis of thought that continues to work against the reunion of these sister disciplines, and in chapter 8 I follow the trends in twentieth-century theology since Teilhard and Tillich, trends that work toward such a reunion. In the dialogue which is now taking place at the interface between science and theology I find that the ground has been prepared for the construction of a new proof for the existence of God, an argument which springs as much from science as from theology, a proof more powerful and compelling than all the old proofs put together.

1.
ALBERT EINSTEIN
New Proof for the Existence of God

NEW PROOF FOR THE EXISTENCE OF GOD

Princeton – Scientists announce new proof for the existence of God. Theologians, philosophers, and the public
are stunned as centuries old debate is ended. Nuclear
physicists at the Institute for Advanced Study at Princeton, New Jersey, held a press conference yesterday to report a major breakthrough in theoretical physics. A
spokesman for the research group, Dr. Kyle Sweden-
borg, told reporters, "It may seem incredible, but our
evidence clearly points to a theory of the universe which
supports the tenets of traditional religion. In other
words, we may have found new proof for the existence
of God."

Of course, these headlines are fiction. There has been no
such news conference at Princeton, nor will there be in the fore-
seeable future. The scientists aren't even looking for God, and,
if such an announcement were made at a prestigious center of
science, the press would double check to be certain it wasn't all
a hoax. This is one of the reasons God is so seldom in the news
these days, but more importantly it is illustrative of a crisis at the
very center of western culture.

Whatever one's opinion about God, it is clear the Judeo-
Christian faith is a structural element in western culture. This is
particularly true in America. Whether one considers the deist
God of the founding fathers or the pietistic God of more contemporary presidents, belief in God has been and continues to
be a phenomenon of the American way of life. Today, however,
God floats on a sea of popular sentiment without a particular
anchor in the life of the mind. People grasp at faith, hoping to
find a source of clarity and truth in the midst of the bewildering
changes in every region of their lives, but there are so many
diffuse and vacuous concepts of God in currency that the in-

quiring mind may simply be bewildered by the multiplicity of choices. Given the host of denominations and the profusion of sects, how is one to distinguish the true from the false? Within Christianity itself the central symbols of the Bible have been cut loose from any coherent theology, and ethics has disintegrated into a random series of debates over topical issues such as abortion or the nuclear arms race. God can be inserted into public discourse at will by politicians, evangelists, talk-show celebrities, or pop psychologists, but there is no view of God which has intellectual substance as well as wide popular appeal. God is not dead. God is suffering the agony of slow dismemberment. Little wonder that institutional religion is not offering the vision and the moral leadership that is so desperately needed by a people confused about the final ends or purposes of life.

As I indicated earlier, the highest achievement of biblical religion is to make possible the unification of consciousness under the rule of a just and loving God. Given contemporary understandings of God and our social disarray, however, it is difficult to imagine that God could be the organizing principle of consciousness for any but a few isolated individuals, let alone for the whole of western society. Nevertheless, there are some hopeful developments to report, some fragmentary fact behind the fiction of my news release. There are concurrent trends in theoretical physics and in theology which may in fact reopen the dialogue between science and religion, make way for a reconciliation of world view with faith, and result in a new concept of God which has both intellectual substance and wide popular appeal. In other words, it may soon be possible to announce the emergence of a new proof for the existence of God.

Still, at this writing, my headline sounds impossible largely because there is an insurmountable barrier of thought separating science and religion. Throughout the twentieth century the world of faith and the world of fact have been seen as completely separate entities. It is the unspoken assumption of most people with a higher education that one's understanding of the material world is shaped without reference to religious conviction. The world of atoms and molecules, forests and trees, stars and planets, this solid world, which can be seen and touched, is the proper subject of scientific investigation whereas religion concerns itself with things unseen, with the world of subjectivity, with the spirit and the soul. Preeminently, religion concerns itself with God. Whatever metaphysical standing one chooses to attribute to God, it is clear that God can neither be touched nor seen. The existence of God can neither be proven nor disproven by scientific research. In this arrangement of reality theology comes out the unquestioned loser, for it is widely assumed that the material world, the world of the scientists, is real while the spiritual world is a matter of pure speculation. Whether one is an atheist, an agnostic, or a devout believer has little bearing upon one's understanding of what is real. A rock, for example, is real. God, on the other hand, is a matter of personal faith.

When American astronauts first brought rocks and rock fragments back from the surface of the moon, most people could fit that fact into a ready-made frame of reference. Rocks belong to the world of fact even if the boundaries of the factual world extend to the moon, to the distant planets, to the stars, or to the reaches of space which have not been touched or seen. Rocks are part of the whole realm of certifiable, verifiable reality. Yet, when the same American astronauts invoked the name of God during their Apollo adventures, there was a tone of condescension in the reporting of it. Moon rocks are real; religious experiences in outer space are a matter of pure speculation.

This apparently self-evident distinction has been undermined by recent developments in science and by concurrent developments in theology. The evolution within the physical sciences can be dramatized by reference to the work of Albert Einstein. Einstein biographers trace his scientific awakening to the earliest years of his childhood. In his autobiographical notes he writes about a formative experience that occurred when he was only five years old. He saw a simple magnetic compass and he was fascinated that the needle of the compass would turn invariably north. It seemed to be drawn by a mysterious force, unseen, unfelt by the human senses, but still very real. In seeing the compass, wrote Einstein, "I experienced a miracle."[1] This event of his early childhood set Einstein's imagination to work. In a sense Einstein spent the rest of his life trying to pursue that fact, trying to understand the equally mysterious forces that keep the stars and planets in their courses and determine the path that light rays follow as they proceed to the outer limits of the universe. As he explored these questions Einstein developed an original model of how the universe operates. His speculations were controversial; they seemed wild and fantastic to his contemporaries, but in the spring of 1919, during a total eclipse of the sun, British astronomers, measuring light from distant stars, confirmed his predictions, and Einstein soon became a figure of international acclaim. The *Times* of London declared that his work had overthrown the commonplace certainties of the ages. This will make necessary a new "philosophy of the universe" concluded the *Times*, "a philosophy that will sweep away nearly all that has been accepted as the axiomatic basis of physical thought."[2] Of course, that overstates the case. In fact, Einstein's formulation of relativity theory did not replace classical physics but rather supplemented and expanded it to integrate a still wider range of material reality. Like Isaac Newton before him, Einstein believed that there was an underlying order in creation. He believed that there was something deeper than the passing stream of events. "In every true searcher of nature, there is a kind of religious reverence," he once said. He identified God with those laws, those orderly principles that he believed were operative in the natural world. Though Einstein did not develop his nascent mysticism systematically, students of theology will recognize in his physics a reformulation of the most tenacious of the traditional arguments for the existence of God. There is an intrinsic order or design in creation which points to the preexistence of a Creator. Classic Newtonian physics, which Einstein refined and reformed in this century's most awesome display of scientific genius, squares very well with this traditional argument for the existence of God. "I believe in a God who reveals himself in the orderly harmony of what exists," said Einstein.

That statement could have been elaborated into a full blown, natural theology, but Einstein focused his energy into the development of relativity and quantum theories. A universe of order, harmony, and design found its quintessential expression in the formula, $E = MC^2$. Yet this scientific work, while representing the most advanced expression of classical physics, also contained the seeds of revolutionary change.

Consider once again the moon rocks—safe territory, one would assume, for anyone completely sanguine with the proposition that matter is real. Thanks to our system of universal public education, it is widely believed that moon rock or any other material substance can be broken down to that smallest unit of matter, the atom. Every high school physics student has seen models of the atom that resemble a tiny solar system, electrons rotating like planets around the nucleus, the sun. Einstein helped define the so-called planetary model of the atom, but his relativity and quantum theories have revealed the atom to be far more elusive and mysterious than any of our models imply. We see now that the atom consists of a host of particles, at once too minute and too puzzling in their behavior to measure with the kind of certainty traditionally required in science. Einstein spent his life trying to plumb those underlying laws and forces holding the whole cosmos together. Yet today in most modern physics it is far from clear that we can ever reach behind the passing stream of events to any fundamental reality at all. Rather than seeing the universe governed by a set of immutable laws, contemporary physics suggests that chance plays a much larger role. Different particles ride different waves of probability. There is an element of unpredictability in all things material. On close examination our proverbial moon rock dissolves into a set of wavelike patterns, so that one can equally well view the rock as a solid, material object and as a continuous, vibrating pattern of pure energy. Its subatomic particles dance and move at ferocious velocities in the vast theater of hypothetical space. As one attempts to apply common sense assumptions about the material world at the outer limits of scientific investigation, even the most basic models break down, revealing an external world which is fundamentally mysterious, unseen and unknown, perhaps unknowable, just like God.

In the early 1920s Einstein was increasingly troubled by the new trends in quantum theory. If the fundamental forces of nature remain beyond the reach of an all-embracing law or theory, then science has no access to reality itself. Also, the God of nature must appear as arbitrary or capricious. During this period Einstein talked so much about God with such obvious conviction to so many scientists that many thought him to be preoccupied with religion. Almost without exception the major scientists with whom Einstein collaborated over his long career recorded their reactions to his beliefs and often offered their own opinions in reply. The record of that protracted debate could be the most important contribution in this century to our understanding of reality. It ranks with the disputes between Luther and Erasmus over free will and determinism. Typically, when Einstein was pressed to uphold his side of the argument against persistent and repeated questioning, the great scientific genius of modern times would fall back upon his faith: "God is subtle, but not malicious," he would affirm; or, more directly, "God does not play dice with the world." In the end, some observers began to feel that even Einstein's great intellect was being sacrificed in defense of an arcane God.

One autumn evening in 1927 the world's leading physicists gathered to talk a little theology after a day-long conference in Brussels, Belgium. During the day they were exploring the mysteries of the new quantum mechanics, but at night they were rattling on about God. Remarked one of the physicists, "Einstein keeps talking about God: what are we to make of that? It is extremely difficult to imagine that a scientist like Einstein should have such strong ties with a religious tradition."[3] Thus Werner Heisenberg (Nobel Prize, 1932) remembers the opening comment in what was to become a debate carried on informally between these giants of modern physics over a period of several decades. The first to offer an explanation, not only for the tenacity of religion in Einstein's thought but also for its persistence in culture generally, was the British physicist, Paul Dirac (Nobel Prize, 1933). As paraphrased by Heisenberg, Dirac's comments represent a bald statement of "scientific atheism," that variety of atheism in which God is put down in the name of science without, however, any actual support from scientific research:

> If we are honest—and scientists have to be—we must admit that religion is a jumble of false assertions, with no basis in reality. The very idea of God is a product of the human imagination. It is quite understandable why primitive people, who were so much more exposed to the overpowering forces of nature than we are today, should have personified these forces in fear and trembling. But nowadays, when we understand so many natural processes, we have no need for such solutions. I can't for the life of me see how the postulate of an Almighty God helps us in any way. What I do see is that this assumption leads to such unproductive questions as why God allows so much misery and injustice, the exploitation of the poor by the rich and all the other horrors He might have prevented. If religion is still being taught, it is by no means because its ideas still convince us, but simply because some of us want to keep the lower classes quiet.[4]

Dirac moves rather quickly here from the position of Freud (that God is merely a personification of the impersonal forces of nature) to the opinion of Marx (that religion is the opiate of the people), but one notices no attempt to support these assertions in any theory or finding of physics. Interestingly, Dirac's putdown of religion did not elicit support from that group of physicists. The conversation moved on a more positive footing until the very end of the evening when Wolfgang Pauli (Nobel Prize, 1945) concluded cryptically, "Well, our friend Dirac, too, has a religion, and its guiding principle is: 'There is no God and Dirac is His prophet.'"[5]

Earlier in the evening, Pauli had made an important distinction between the views of Einstein and those of Max Planck (Nobel Prize, 1918). Planck was also noted for his frequent faith statements but, it was agreed, Planck removed the very possibility of conflict between science and religion by setting them apart into two entirely different domains: the subjective and the objective. Religion in Planck's view deals with the dimension of human values, with the workings of the soul and the spirit, while science deals with the factual and the material, the operations of logic and reason. Thus, it could be agreed, within the context of this after-hours discussion, that Max Planck's affirmation of the Christian faith was no more pertinent than Paul Dirac's denials. Neither view is contiguous with the actual research being carried on in the natural sciences. Moreover, one might conclude that religion has more to fear from such friends than it has to fear from the direct attacks by its enemies like Dirac. For the God whom Max Planck affirms is a God fated to die the death of a thousand qualifications. To defend religion by carving up reality so as to leave certain realms to science and certain realms to religion is a well-intended maneuver that in one stroke eliminates the possibility that God can be what God must be; namely, the organizing principle of reality itself. When there is real conflict between science and religion, it is far preferable to face it directly. As a matter of fact, all people of faith should pray that there is some conflict with science, for where there is no conflict there can be no room for agreement either. The central question is this: does that picture of reality which emerges from science square with the picture of reality which is part of one's religious experience? If there is a consistent, coherent, and compelling view of the world that is rooted in scientific research as well as in religious experience, then one has a far deeper confidence than if one's understanding is informed by either science or religion alone. The late-night discussion in that Brussels hotel room was so heated precisely because Einstein saw a direct threat to his faith in the scientific theories being put forward so enthusiastically by his colleagues. Einstein was not concerned about, he was not even interested in, the polemics of "scientific atheism," but he was deeply concerned that certain findings at the frontier of physics seemed to undercut everything he believed about nature's God.

Einstein's self-chosen mission in life was to illuminate and explicate to his generation the orderly processes of nature. He passionately believed that knowledge of that order puts one directly in touch with God. His famous formula and the whole of relativity theory are practically a hymn to the God of order and reason. Contrary to popular opinion, Einstein had not reduced the force of law in nature by making all things relative. Rather, he showed the interrelationship of all things in nature to the one, final constant: the speed of light. All energy and matter, time and space, past, present, and future, all revolved around this one unchanging fact. It is, of course, more than coincidental that light is the most ancient and traditional of all symbols for God. In the sometimes paradoxical behavior of light, relativity theory, like religion, finds a key that unlocks some of nature's deepest secrets. Hence Einstein saw a deep correspondence between science and religion and an interrelated purpose for them both. "Science without religion is lame, religion without science is blind," he once said.

In his work Einstein had overturned many of our most basic preconceptions about the world. He demonstrated that the mystical order which Isaac Newton had seen in the universe is at once more far-reaching and radically simple than Newton had ever dreamed. Yet the process of rethinking and reshaping the very structures of understanding which Einstein started did not stop with Einstein, and he could not control the direction which his colleagues were taking as they pursued his own ideas. Under the leadership of Niels Bohr (Nobel Prize, 1922) many of the physicists meeting that night in Brussels had seen the very order of the cosmos called into question. One could no longer construct a clear or complete picture of the atom. Instead of a simple model the scientists were encountering strange and mysterious oscillations of energy. They were seeing particles with movements so rapid and changes so sudden, spontaneous, and unpredictable that they seemed to be disappearing across the horizons of understanding. At the level of subatomic particles one could make measurements, collect data, and calculate probabilities, but one could not with certainty predict future events. With the past, present, and future turning circles around each other, everything suddenly seemed to be up for grabs. It seemed like the very notion of a solid, physical world was vanishing like so much smoke in the wind.

Ironically, the initial conclusion drawn by the London *Times* had proven itself valid, though for completely different reasons and contrary to Einstein's understanding of his own work. His theories had been extrapolated in such a way that they swept away "nearly all that has been accepted as the axiomatic basis of physical thought." The debate started in the Brussels hotel was continued over the next several decades in scientific journals, personal correspondence, lectures, and books. What has emerged is the realization that our relationship to the material world is as problematic as our relationship with God. Matter, that solid, quantifiable, definite object of scientific investigation, has been exposed for what it really is: a mystery beyond human understanding. Consequently we have, for example, Professor John Wheeler of the University of Texas at Austin writing lines like these: "What we have been accustomed to call 'physical reality' turns out to be largely a *papier mâché* construction of our imagination plastered between our observations. In fact, these human observations constitute the only reality we know."[6] Dr. Fritjof Capra of Berkeley writes, "At the subatomic level, matter does not exist with certainty at definite places, but rather shows 'tendencies to exist.'"[7]

It is curious that the two major problems associated with belief in God have also proven to be problems inherent in our commonsense attitudes toward the material world. Philosophers have undercut the foundations of traditional theism by showing that one's observations of the world cannot be extrapolated into generalized statements about ultimate reality and that such statements, if attempted, can only be conceived as projections of one's personal experience into hypothetical space. Now, in the closing decades of the twentieth century we are finding that the moon rock is as much a matter of doubt as God.

A number of years ago in theological circles it was widely accepted that one could not rely with confidence upon a "God of the gaps." It was a self-defeating undertaking for defenders of the faith to identify God with those unresolved questions, those gaps in the ever-expanding universe of human knowledge. For with science steadily advancing upon the great mysteries all the gaps would sooner or later be filled in, and there would no longer be a theoretical need for God. Now the tables are being turned: as scientists expand the range of their vision and the circle of their knowledge, the gaps become wider and wider. Today it is literally the case that as our knowledge increases so does our awareness of those still larger regions yet unknown. In a very real sense our ignorance is growing faster than our knowledge. Above all, we are seeing that there has always been an element of metaphysical hubris in our certainty about the material world.

Meanwhile, at the frontiers of theology, there have been equally radical transformations. While it is still popularly assumed that the essence of theism is belief in a supernatural being, the fundamental distinction between the natural and the supernatural has been dismantled. To assert the existence of a being who exists above and beyond the laws of nature becomes increasingly irrelevant as the "laws of nature" are themselves exposed as mental constructs. Also, if God is conceived as a being alongside all other finite beings, then God is no longer God. This new situation requires a new understanding of theism itself.

Paul Tillich was the first major theologian to see the radical implications of this predicament. As he repeatedly pointed out, it becomes nonsensical in this context to discuss the existence or nonexistence of God. Religious teachings about God can only be regarded as one way of making sense of the apparently incoherent array of facts that present themselves to human consciousness. The word *God*, like the formula $E = MC^2$, is essentially a symbol through which one can express a sense of order, harmony, and mystical union with . . . what? Of course, that question is yet unanswered. It is the point at which science and religion converge on the frontier of consciousness. For, aside from the immediate facts which present themselves through our senses, all we really have are the symbols—"*papier mâché* constructions," if you will, "plastered between our observations." Religious and scientific symbols are equally problematic when it comes to pursuing that most basic of all human questions: what is real?

Ironically, however, religious symbols may prove to be more appropriate in this situation than are popular scientific symbols, for, while it is naively assumed that we have definite and final knowledge about the material world, people are generally prepared to admit that they do not possess direct knowlege of God. There has always been an element of skepticism, self-criticism, and theological humility built into the Judeo-Christian tradition. Theologians have characteristically stopped short of the claim that they have seen God "face to face." In fact, the biblical prohibition against idols and icons represents an element of philosophical caution even in the midst of the most immodest tradition.

Moreover, traditional religious conceptions have already been freed from the deadly grip of literalism because they are continually tested by experience in a way that scientific conceptions are not. The age of astronomy and space exploration has exposed the vast majority of religious people to the realization that the deity does not reside in a kingdom somewhere "up there." Experience with pain and suffering and an awareness of evil and injustice on a global scale continue to raise the most basic challenge to traditional theism; namely, how can an all-powerful and loving God permit such tragedy and injustice to continue? Most recently, the feminist movement has raised renewed doubts about a God who is conceived primarily as a man. In response to these challenges theologians have recourse to a rich history of symbolic elaboration in which God is conceived in more subtle and suggestive terms than the critics of the tradition presume.

Even in the biblical conception the faces and moods and forms of God are infinitely varied. God is seen in the light of the sun, in the cloud and thunder of the storm. Yet biblical literature stops short of equating God with these natural phenomena. God is heard in the voice of a stranger one meets on a lonely road or in the fierce words of a prophet. God is recognized in the innocence of a baby lying in a manger or in the pain of a man hanging on a cross, near death, but the people in whom God is seen and heard are not treated as gods. God is known in the work of reason, in the depth of emotion, or in the appearance of beauty, but God is not identified with these human experiences. God is depicted in an endless variety of shapes and forms, but no image of God is fully or finally complete. We stand in relation to God as the scientist stands before the universe, only beginning to scratch the surface of understanding. In this respect we are all in the position of the five-year-old Einstein who set out to resolve the miracle of the magnet. We proceed in the undertaking of science and theology armed only with faith that understanding is possible. We hope that the pattern of the seashell or the turn of a season is not simply a random constellation of order in the midst of chaos. We believe, but we do not know.

Yet as we search the surface of things, as scientists and theologians follow their separate paths of investigation, a similar image of reality seems to be taking shape. On the one hand, modern physics pictures the universe as a web of interrelationships in which the distinctions between time and space, energy and matter, fact and theory are neither so clear nor so final as we once believed. As scientists reflect upon the material world it becomes apparent that the universe does not consist of isolated components but rather appears to be a complex set of relationships which fit together into a unified whole.

Likewise, on the frontiers of theology, God is seen not as a separate being who dwells somewhere up there; rather, theologians are now seeing God as being directly involved in a continuing process of creation. As the physicists have found in nature, so also in God the distinctions vanish between time and space, spirit and matter, temporal and eternal. Now for scientists and theologians alike the universe is seen as a dynamic, mysterious, paradoxical process, and in moments of mystical illumination the vast array of observations is fused together into a unified whole. At the outer edges of perception human consciousness is integrated under the rule of a just and loving God.

What had threatened Einstein so deeply about modern physics was the idea that the universe evolves through a random process. At the subatomic level basic interactions are unpredictable and seem to be shaped by chance. To Einstein such a view seemed to preclude the rule of law and to remove one's anchor to reality itself. That is what he meant when he referred to the statistical interpretation of quantum mechanics as "this fundamental dice game." Yet, the God of order and design was a product more of Greek philosophy than of biblical religion. The new physics does not conflict with the God of the Bible, but instead reopens the door of faith. For the God of Abraham, Isaac, and Jacob, the God of Jesus was also believed to be unpredictable and inscrutable, that is to say, "beyond human reckoning." Belief in such a God does not rule out the element of spontaneity, freedom, and surprise in the universe. In fact, it is precisely the personal God of the Judeo-Christian tradition which squares most accurately with that view of the world that has emerged from physics. Many popular interpreters of science have missed this point precisely because of the confusion between Greek philosophy and biblical religion. A whole literature has emerged suggesting that Eastern religion offers the true opportunity for dialogue between science and theology. Books like Fritjof Capra's *The Tao of Physics* and Gary Zukav's *The Dancing Wu Li Masters* have advanced the suggestion that quantum mechanics is a modern-day equivalent for the mysticism of the East. These commentators, however, seem to be writing in blissful ignorance of both the Bible and trends in western theology. Today's theologians, Protestant, Catholic, and Jewish, are rediscovering their roots in the Bible even as they are being informed by the latest scientific understandings.

As presently conceived at the frontiers of theology, belief in God is not antithetical to scientific inquiry; rather, there is a distinct possibility that scientists and theologians may again fuse the disparate elements of their separate worlds into a single vision of the whole. In fact, the prospect of such a synthesis of science and religion is one of the most promising frontiers of the imagination. In such a reunification of consciousness God will be seen, not alone in the order and harmony of the natural world, but in the paradox, complexity, and ultimate mystery as well. Thus the argument from design in nature shall be supplemented by its own mirror image; and the hidden symmetry between the scientific and the theological shall be revealed. When this is accomplished a new element of plausibility and persuasiveness shall be evident in the symbols of faith. In the closing years of the twentieth century physicists will continue searching for a superunification theory, and theologians will re-examine and refine the ancient symbols of "the one." At the same time, both will borrow from the work being done in related disciplines. When the human imagination can free itself from the inhibiting assumptions of a secular age, then western culture may enter a period of creativity unparalleled in modern times. It is quite possible that the opening years of the twenty-first century may be known as the new age of God. During this new era, Einstein's early credo may become the confession of all true searchers of nature: "Science without religion is lame; religion without science is blind."

2.
SIGMUND FREUD
Where Illusion Meets Reality

Sigmund Freud was perhaps the most persuasive advocate for atheism in this century. Though he was not the first to suggest that God is a mere product and figment of the human imagination, he drew fresh support for this view from his own research into the depths of human consciousness. Writing in the opening decades of the century, Freud framed the argument against God in such a way that he seemed to strike at the very weakest and most vulnerable point in the armature of faith. Especially for a generation educated according to Victorian standards, the proposition that belief in God is a product of infantile sex fantasies proved to be sufficiently provocative that the church has yet to recover from the shock waves which his theories set loose. Now in the 1980s, while many of Freud's basic teachings have become an accepted part of pop psychology, it is clear that most religious people have yet to grasp the significance of his assertions. Still shackled by its own fears about sex, the church has yet to digest the arguments he put forward, let alone advance a positive alternative to what may now be the prevailing view of religion for several generations who have studied depth psychology since the 1920s and 1930s. The continuing defensiveness and naiveté of the churches toward sexuality only reinforce the impression that faith has more to fear than it has to learn from an honest exploration into the deepest mysteries of human life.

Nothing could be more misguided or mistaken than this defensiveness for, as we shall see, a rigorous and courageous pursuit of the ideas articulated by Freud and his successors in the psychoanalytic profession leads not to the destruction of faith but to its rebirth and renewal. In fact, a deeper appreciation for Freud's criticisms of religion may prepare the church for a period of unprecedented creativity. Equally important, a critical pursuit of Freud's insight into the relationship between spirituality and sexuality may remove the single most important obstacle to awareness of God's presence in the world.

Freud's basic statement concerning the role of religion is set forward clearly and unequivocally in *The Future of an Illusion* (1927). In this short, tightly written study (one might almost say, tract) Freud spells out what has become the most familiar of contemporary arguments against God. He begins with this moving account of the terrors inflicted upon humanity by the untamed forces of nature:

> There are the elements, which seem to mock at all human control: the earth, which quakes and is torn apart and buries all human life and its works; water, which deluges and drowns everything in a turmoil; storms, which blow everything before them; there are diseases, which we have only recently recognized as attacks by other organisms; and finally there is the painful riddle of death, against which no medicine has yet been found, nor probably will be. With these forces nature rises up against us, majestic, cruel and inexorable; she brings to our mind once more our weakness and helplessness, which we thought to escape through the work of civilization.[1]

Freud argues that it is the principal task of civilization to defend against these "cold, cruel, and relentless forces." Chief among the strategies for coping with such primeval terror is religion. Since nature leaves humanity helpless before its awesome power, people attempt to transform the impersonal forces of nature into personal beings with whom one can communicate and to whom one can appeal for mercy. One can, in fact, apply the same methods in relating to the violence of nature that one would use against an overpowering human opponent; one can "try to adjure them, to appease them, to bribe them, and, by so influencing them . . . rob them of a part of their power."[2]

Freud then draws an analogy between the human condition itself and the individual predicament of every human infant:

> Once before one has found oneself in a similar state of helplessness: as a small child, in relation to one's parents. One had reason to fear them, and especially one's father; and yet one was

> sure of his protection against the dangers one knew. . . . In the
> same way, a man makes the forces of nature not simply into
> persons with whom he can associate as he would with his
> equals—that would not do justice to the overpowering impres-
> sion which those forces make on him—but he gives them the
> character of a father.[3]

Hence the God of the Judeo-Christian tradition arises out of the
terror and helplessness of humanity. The whole enterprise of
religion represents an exact repetition of the infant's response
to the awesome presence of its own parents. Freud summarizes
these conclusions in *Civilization and Its Discontents* (1929):

> The common man cannot imagine this Providence otherwise
> than in the figure of an enormously exalted father. Only such a
> being can understand the needs of the children of men and be
> softened by their prayers and placated by the signs of their re-
> morse. The whole thing is so patently infantile, so foreign to
> reality, that to anyone with a friendly attitude to humanity it is
> painful to think that the great majority of mortals will never be
> able to rise above this view of life.[4]

It is not surprising that people of faith reacted strongly and
harshly to such criticisms. Freud was well aware that an analysis
of religion which reduces it to the status of neurosis and explains
its powers over the human imagination as an obsession was not
calculated to promote cordial dialogue with the world's religious
leaders. Nor was his writing intended to win him friends in the
religious community. He was fully conscious of the costs, both
personal and professional, that might follow the publication of
such a critique of religion. Nevertheless, he pursued this train
of thought and put forward his critique of the Judeo-Christian
God as being, in essence, a reappearance in adult life of the all-
powerful figure which every child encounters in its own father.
For Freud, the return of the repressed father figure in the form
of an omnipotent father-God explains both the power of religion within the individual's life and its persistence within western culture as a whole.

Before looking at the flaws which have since become evident
in Freud's analysis of religion, it is crucial to affirm the truth and

accuracy of his observations. For many people God does seem
to be little more than an inflated image of their own biological
father or an expression of deep longing for a father figure which
was felt to be lacking in early childhood. To the extent that faith
in God is the product of neurosis, to the extent that the father
God is held to with the blind devotion one might expect in an
obsession, Freud's insights offer a much needed antidote to a
negative and repressive religion. His insights are most helpful,
however, not to the enemies of faith but to faith itself in providing a basis for distinguishing between idolatry and authentic
religion. Clearly the health and even the survival of theism quite
literally depend upon the successful purging away of all forms
of faith in which God is merely a magnified image of one's biological father. Freud's lasting contribution to the evolution of
religion is precisely in providing a more effective diagnostic tool
for distinguishing between wishful fantasies and actual experiences of the holy.

Whatever the merits of Freud's critique, it is clear that his use
of the word *infantile* in the passage cited above was polemical.
Similarly, many of the rather technical terms of psychoanalytic
theory take a negative connotation when used with reference to
religion. Taking Freud's analysis of culture on its own terms and
at face value, such a bias against religion is not justified. For, as
Freud sees it, civilization itself arises out of the same fear and
helplessness that gave rise to theism. "I have tried to show that
religious ideas have arisen from the same need as have all the
other achievements of civilization."[5] Art and literature, ethics
and morality, philosophy, and even science represent at bottom
an attempt to find meaning and gratification in the midst of
nature's terror. If religion can be seen as an attempt to create
some sense of compensation for satisfactions lacking in reality,
so too can all other aspects of culture. Even science falls under
the shadow of this analysis. As Freud puts it in *Civilization and
Its Discontents:*

> Life, as it is imposed on us, is too hard for us: it brings us too
> many hurts, disappointments, insoluble tasks. To endure it, we
> cannot do without palliatives. . . . There are perhaps three such

means: powerful diversions which make us esteem our misery
lightly, substitute gratifications which lessen it, and intoxicants
which render us insensitive. Something of this sort is indispensable. . . . All scientific activity, too, is such a diversion.[6]

Essentially Freud argues that religion tries to divert humanity from the suffering of life by turning its back on reality. Having insisted that civilization itself is one grand diversion,
however, it is difficult to find in the logic of this analysis any basis
for distinguishing between what is helpful diversion (e.g., science) and harmful delusion (e.g., religion). We must then ask,
what explains the intensity of Freud's attack upon religion; why,
in other words, does his objective analysis disintegrate into hostile polemic when he addresses the problem of faith? Short of
speculating about the role of the unconscious in Freud's own
mental life, there is a great deal of evidence to suggest that he
realized religion offered a view of the world which contradicted
his own view at crucial points. The question as to the truth or
falsehood of religion, the existence or non-existence of God, was
not merely theoretical. For if the affirmations of religion are
illusory they are at least illusions spun in an attempt to fulfill
"the oldest, strongest, and most urgent wishes of mankind."

Freud was willing to grant that faith arises out of the deepest
needs, is fueled by the strongest desires, and is founded upon
the most powerful instincts of human nature. Faith wrestles, in
other words, with the very dilemmas which his own theories try
to encompass. Yet what if the images of faith convey a more
accurate picture of reality than psychoanalytic theory conveys?
The intensity of Freud's feelings about religion clearly reflect his
sense of confrontation and combat. He played the part of a partisan contestant in a struggle for the souls of humankind, and
he set his own world view in direct contradiction to faith.

It seems not to be the case that there is a Power in the universe
which watches over the well-being of individuals with parental
care and brings all their affairs to a happy ending. On the contrary, the destinies of mankind can be brought into harmony
neither with the hypothesis of a Universal Benevolence nor with
the partly contradictory one of a Universal Justice. Earthquakes,

tidal waves, conflagrations, make no distinction between the vir-
tuous and pious and the scoundrel or unbeliever. Even where
what is in question is not inanimate Nature but where an individual's fate depends on his relations to other people, it is by no
means the rule that virtue is rewarded and that evil finds its
punishment. Often enough the violent, cunning or ruthless
man seizes the envied good things of the world and the pious
man goes away empty. Obscure, unfeeling and unloving powers
determine men's fate.[7]

The question must be raised whether Freud had any greater
justification for his assertions that the universe is governed by
"obscure, unfeeling and unloving powers" than theists have in
affirming the universe is governed by a just and loving God.
Freud's negative assessment of religion is at bottom a negative
assessment about life itself. His assertion that human life is
shaped by hostile powers may just as easily be described as an
inflation of his personal experience to the status of an assertion
about ultimate reality. Of course, the suggestion that one builds
faith from the ground up, so to speak, is not particularly revolutionary or even controversial. In fact, even greater problems
would be presented by a faith which is not grounded in one's
personal experience. The question then remains whether any
faith or world view can be shown to square with reality. In this
respect atheism must pass exactly the same test as theism.

This brings us to Freud's view of human sexuality and the
source of his deep skepticism. When he asserted that the erotic
instincts lie at the root of human consciousness, his views startled
a generation which had been reared in almost total silence on
this topic. When he advanced his theory that sex is the key to
human identity, many of his contemporaries reacted with shock
and disbelief. According to Freud, one can explain all human
achievement as a form of erotic energy redirected into another
sphere. As we have seen, art and architecture, sports and fashion, science and, of course, religion are really little more than
reconstituted sexuality. Despite the element of novelty in these
views, Freud believed, like the Victorians of his own era, that sex
was a dangerous force. If allowed free reign, the erotic impulses
would run rampant, ultimately bringing an end to civilization

itself. By way of illustration, consider Freud's description of what would happen if restrictions against sexual expression were lifted:

> If one imagines its prohibitions lifted—if, then, one may take any woman one pleases as a sexual object, if one may without hesitation kill one's rival for her love or anyone else who stands in one's way, if, too, one can carry off any of the other man's belongings without asking leave—how splendid, what a string of satisfactions one's life would be! True, one soon comes across the first difficulty: everyone else has exactly the same wishes as I have and will treat me with no more consideration than I treat him. And so in reality only one person could be made unrestrictedly happy by such a removal of the restrictions of civilization, and he would be a tyrant, a dictator, who had seized all the means to power. And even he would have every reason to wish that the others would observe at least one cultural commandment: 'thou shalt not kill'.[8]

Even the Puritans in their darkest hours did not have a more negative view of the erotic. At the same time, however, Freud insisted that the libido was in fact the motivating and energizing force behind all human behavior. The secret to human creativity was to redirect the erotic instinct toward a higher object. Rather than allowing its individual members free reign to act out their desires, society functions by putting erotic energy in service to a socially desirable end and purpose. This process, which Freud called sublimation, is the cornerstone of psychoanalytic theory, and it has proven to be an invaluable contribution to our knowledge of how the human mind actually works. In sum, Freud was able to explain in clear and concrete terms the interconnecting tissue of human consciousness itself. He was able to show how the experiences of earliest childhood could influence behavior in later life; he was able to reveal the interrelationship between the conflicting thoughts and contradictory feelings that are part of all our lives. He developed an explanation of how our conscious life is related to and often influenced by the unconscious. He was able to account for many of the inconsistencies, cross-purposes, paradoxes, and simple errors that are a normal part of human behavior. At the same time, he greatly expanded human understanding of abnormal and aberrant behavior. His insights have been invaluable in the treatment of mental disease of all kinds; his methods of treatment represent the single most important contribution to mental health in this century. In other words, Freud rightly deserves his reputation as the father of depth psychology, and his contributions to our understanding of the human mind place him at the very pinnacle of intellectual achievement.

It is therefore all the more ironic that Freud devoted more and more of his own energy to the study of religion in his later years. In his later writings his chief preoccupation is religion even though he had rendered his negative assessment very early in his career. Again and again he repeated his view that God was an illusion that would inevitably lose its hold upon the human imagination just as Santa Claus or the stork are dismissed when the child realizes the truth behind these myths of early childhood. To the end he persisted in the view that the promises of religion and the affirmations of theism simply do not square with reality. Yet, in the elaboration and development of his own theories, Freud was quite clearly on the trail of an insight which leads through the doors opened by depth psychology itself to a new appreciation for the insights of religion. The very operations of the human mind which Freud so brilliantly illuminated may confirm the most basic, biblical affirmations about creation.

If we follow this trail and pursue Freud's own insights to their logical conclusion, we may gain a deeper appreciation for the symmetry between science and religion. As we combine the insights of depth psychology with the biblical account of creation, we may reach a still more accurate understanding of life's deepest mysteries. The trail which leads from the depths of human consciousness toward a rediscovery of God is precisely that element of Freud's thinking which at first seems most threatening to faith; namely, the importance he attached to the erotic. In his later writing Freud refined his theory of the erotic substantially. Still insisting that all forms of human behavior have their roots in the sex instincts, Freud began to shift his understanding of the erotic in one crucial respect.

From the beginning Freud had tried to show that the erotic drives were not simply geared toward genital union between partners of the opposite sex. Freud saw that there is a more general role for sexuality: the erotic drives provide the motive power behind all manner of human activity having nothing whatever to do with the reproductive process. When he tried to explain the all-pervasive presence of the erotic, Freud reached back into Greek mythology, and he reached forward to the frontiers of modern chemistry and physics to theorize that there is a "chemical affinity" in all inanimate matter analogous to the affinity between men and women.[9] In fact, the erotic drive is, for Freud, rooted in the chemical and physical makeup of all matter; in living tissue it appears as a tendency to "combine organic substances into ever larger unities." In this way, concludes Freud, "the libido of our sexual instincts would coincide with the Eros of the poets and philosophers which binds all living things together."[10] In his later work Freud spoke of the larger social purposes of the erotic:

> I may now add that civilization is a process in the service of Eros, whose purpose is to combine single human individuals, and after that families, then races, peoples and nations, into one great unity, the unity of mankind.[11]

Freud went far afield to find precedents for this conclusion; he went as far back as 800 BC to the ancient Hindu Scriptures, the Upanishad. Curiously, Freud did not search for parallels in the Bible even though the Scriptures of his own religious tradition offer a more direct and obvious model for his own concept of the erotic. Had he been capable of overcoming his own antagonism toward religion, he may have seen that "the Eros of the poets and philosophers" is compatible with that other form of love which the Greeks called Agape, the love of God. At a level of analysis still deeper than that which Freud was able to attain, the sexual and the spiritual forms of love are fused under the rule of a just and loving God.

Though Freud saw himself as a champion of human liberation over and against the repressive attitudes of religion, his

understanding of human sexuality retained much of the nega-
tivism that was characteristic of the Victorian era. Though he
fought to broaden popular definitions of sexuality and succeeded beyond any reasonable expectation in doing just that for
the several generations following him, still he never overcame
his sense of antagonism between the sex drives and the higher
ends and purposes of civilization. He continued to see human
culture arising out of its roots in the erotic in such a way that
there was a continuing and constant tension between the higher
and lower impulses of the human spirit. Herbert Marcuse articulates the central problem of Freud's theory in his own study,
Eros and Civilization. He points out that if every form of social
and cultural life is built on a foundation of repressed sexuality,
then it is impossible to envision a non-repressive society. The
libidinal drives must be repressed and redirected so that more
enduring forms of love may emerge. However, if we follow the
clues which Freud left in his later work and fuse them with the
understanding of sexuality in the biblical account of creation,
then the foundation is established for a truly positive, truly liberating notion of the erotic. More importantly, the inner compatibility of the erotic and the religious drives can be
appreciated perhaps for the first time. One can then attain a
new sense of the symmetry between the psychological and the
theological, and one can find within the hidden dynamics of
human consciousness new support for the authenticity of faith.

The biblical account of creation affirms two points pertinent
to this discussion. First, humanity is created in the image of God
as male and female. Second, at the very moment of creation
humanity enjoys at one and the same time sexual union and
union with the Creator. In the creation story, life is stripped to
its essence; in the garden of Eden, there were none of the trap-
pings of advanced civilization; in the beginning there were no
museums, no factories, no fast-food restaurants, no schools, no
churches, and certainly no religion. Humankind was created in
the image of God, male and female. There is a stark simplicity
in the creation story emphasizing what is of paramount importance. There were two primary elements in the life of this man

and this woman: the erotic drive which held them together as a couple and the religious drive that kept them close to God. Eros and Agape were not differentiated and certainly not antagonistic. For Adam and Eve sexuality and spirituality were not mutually exclusive, but rather complementary and mutually supportive. Thus Genesis anticipates Freud by emphasizing the importance of sex, but it avoids his costly mistake by showing that the physical and the spiritual drives work together as the highest and, at the same time, the deepest processes of life.

Unfortunately most interpreters of the Bible, including Freud, have read Genesis backwards, emphasizing both the fall of humanity from this state of grace and the antagonisms which have characterized all human relationships since the fall rather than stressing the positive insights conveyed by the creation story itself. Hence the biblical affirmations are lost and sex is seen as a life-threatening force, hostile to the "higher" purposes of culture and religion. Tragically, the positive elements of biblical and Freudian tradition are turned to a wholly negative use. Thus both the Bible and Freud are used as a source of proof-texts by those who still preach an ethic of repression.

Reading the creation story apart from these traditional distortions, one finds that it asserts an inner symmetry between sexuality and spirituality. Adam and Eve are created as sexual beings, free to enjoy each other and their natural surrounding as they live out their destiny in the image of God. God created them, male and female, so that loneliness would be exiled from a world which lacked nothing but love. ("It is not good that the man should be alone" [Gen. 2:18].) Clearly love was primary in the order of creation. That is to say, love of God and love for each other was primary, and procreation was secondary. Taking the imagery of Genesis seriously one can say that human life is complete only when the essential unity of the erotic and the religious life is restored. From a biblical perspective one simply cannot talk about salvation of the soul; one finds salvation in and through the body, in and through a community of believers, in and through reconciliation with all things, animate and inanimate.

This biblical emphasis has often been lost by theologians and other interpreters of the text. The official reading of the creation story limits sex to a subheading under the doctrine of marriage, where it loses its importance and its pivotal position in the totality of life. This tendency is exemplified by St. Paul who implied that even marriage could not contain the dangerous influences of the erotic and that celibacy was the preferred condition. Clearly, in its official teaching, the church has been preoccupied with discussion of the proper *institutional* arrangements between the sexes. In some periods celibacy has been seen as the ideal solution to the threat of the erotic, and in other periods marriage has been put forward as the ideal. I would argue that much of this debate fails to retain the deepest insight of the Bible. In fact, the highest ideal of the Scriptures is neither matrimony nor celibacy but rather a community of persons in which there is a direct, intrinsic connection between the life of the flesh and the life of the spirit.

To speak in these terms is to follow both Freud and Genesis forward to a new definition of the erotic. In its original and most basic form, the erotic is a primordial urge for the unification of that which is separate and apart. The essence of sex is not genital intercourse, but the full knowledge and love of one person for another. In their true meeting human beings are drawn together simultaneously in spiritual and sensual dimensions. Genital contact is only one mode of expressing the erotic drive. The fact that one cannot even discuss sex in this culture without conjuring up images of the promiscuous indicates a fundamental flaw in our vision of the erotic. Hence it is only by a deliberate suspension of preconceptions that one can begin to recapture the biblical insight about sexuality.

According to biblical conception, sexual satisfaction is an intrinsic element in salvation and the church, as the body of Christ is, at least potentially, the erotic community per se. Under the rule of God, physical contact takes on sacramental significance and becomes transparent to the holy. This is an affirmation contained in the tradition on marriage, though often obscured. Even St. Paul reflects this view in his dictum, "Husbands, love

your wives, as Christ loved the church" (Eph. 5:25). In this saying Paul was affirming the reciprocity which is part of any loving
relationship, but Paul's image conveys by implication what his
theology did not permit him to acknowledge directly; namely,
the intrinsic connection between physical and spiritual forms of
love. If it is possible to see the similarity between Christ's love
for the church and a husband's love for his wife, it is also possible
to push the analogy beyond the walls of the church and the
nuclear family. In all encounters between human beings there is
an element of sexuality and spirituality. The challenge is to let
these twins of our selfhood work together for the good of each
person in a particular relationship.

In this context one needs to supplement Paul's dualism with
the more consistently biblical attitude expressed in the Song of
Songs. As the poetry of that book suggests, erotic love is not
limited to marriage; rather it plays a central role in the religious
life itself. Thus, throughout church history and in the face of
the most repressive tendencies, the evocative poetry of that book
has been used interchangeably to depict the love that joins a man
and a woman, Christ and the church, God and humankind.

At this juncture it is critical to recall that there are two primary dimensions of life as it takes shape in the image of God.
Gen. 1—2 precedes Freud by several millennia in placing sexuality at the very center of the riddle of human identity, but
Genesis offers an alternative view in relating sexuality directly to
spirituality and all the higher purposes of life. The biblical image combines both forms of love in its portrait of life under the
rule of God. Yet, from the opening chapters, Genesis tells the
gradually unfolding story of alienation as humanity is divided
against itself—Adam and Eve, Cain and Abel, city of Babel,
Sodom and Gomorrah. The original unity of spirit and flesh,
God and humankind, is gradually replaced by a tragic polarity.
Not only are human beings at war with each other, but also mind
and body are divided against themselves. Increasingly, perversions of sexual identity are associated with perversions of the
spirit.

It was this double-edged quality of evil which Jesus so clearly recognized. With a backward glance at Genesis, Jesus looked forward to a reunion of the physical and spiritual under the rule of God. His obvious affection for the "prostitutes and sinners," his transformation of the Jewish family meal into an open-ended love feast with eschatological dimensions, his insistence that the breaking of bread and the washing of feet were not just symbolic but rather necessary ingredients of salvation itself, and his insistence upon the relationship between physical and spiritual healing, all are signs of a life in which sensuality and spirituality work together for the good. The sensuality of Jesus is as evident and ever-present in the Scriptures as is his spirituality. His feel for the erotic is manifest in the manner of his speech and the style of his parables and stories. Note especially his use of concrete images, his reliance upon metaphors that spring from nature, his emphasis upon relationships that cross the normal boundaries and conventions of society. Above all, one must note his identification of "the scribes and pharisees" as the opposite party to the prostitutes in the dialectic of evil. Jesus seemed to be aware that it is repressive morality which defines sex as evil and thereby makes prostitution profitable.

As we have seen, the genius of Freud was to illuminate the role of the erotic in all human experiences. His insights into the all-pervasive reach of the erotic is indispensable to a comprehensive and constructive view of sex, even though his theories themselves preserve the negative evaluation of the erotic current in his own culture. What Freud accomplished for sex, the doctrine of creation can achieve for the spirit, affirming the presence of God in the material world. From this perspective it is apparent that negative attitudes about the erotic which we still encounter in the churches represent a denial of creation in the name of the Creator. For Christians this is particularly tragic, since the doctrine of creation is reinforced by the doctrine of the incarnation. What that miracle means is quite simply that the love of God takes human shape. In the act of atonement God's presence is made real at the level of the physical and sensual. If, therefore, depth psychology reveals the erotic roots of religious experience, theology can and should expose the hidden religious elements in the life of the senses. In essence, the Freudian analysis of experience can be turned upon itself to expose the mystical dimensions of life in the flesh. For, at heart, all human experience is replete with signs of the divine presence.

When read through the mirror of the creation story, it is apparent that all forms of sexual expression are merely repressed spirituality. Even the most hedonistic forms of behavior reflect the energy of God, albeit redirected and disguised in secular form. In all times and in various ways people have felt that the erotic life is only an arduous seeking after one's final destiny in God, a searching for the reunion of what has been separated under the rule of a just and loving God. The fleeting illusion of union in the sex act itself is normally followed by a reaction, a retreat, a sense of incompletion. How often a painful sense of dissatisfaction afflicts those who have claimed for themselves sexual liberation without first seeking liberation of the spirit. This is the tragic lesson learned by so many who live in the aftermath of the sexual revolution, a revolution which failed only because it was not radical enough. A thoroughgoing transformation of society must involve a reunion of the flesh with the spirit. A complete picture of those forces and counterforces at work in American society today must include Freud's insights into the erotic roots of all culture, as well as the biblical sense of the hidden religious content in all human experience.

Conventional criticisms of American society include the observation that the production and use of consumer goods and services are all-pervasive and all-important. In many respects that is an accurate observation; Americans do see the pursuit of happiness as an undertaking which can succeed only in an environment of extreme affluence. Thus, an all-pervasive "materialism" is seen to compete with the official morality of traditional religion. Yet such an analysis obscures the actual crisis of identity which is the central problem of this culture.

Though the production of consumer goods and services is a central activity of industrial society, it is curious that the felt desire for possessions must be constantly intensified through mass advertising. In this advertising, sex is quite self-consciously and deliberately used as the most effective means of selling the manufacturer's product. In the imagery of the marketplace, men and women are transformed into sex objects, and objects become the personified figures of identity, value, and meaning. Out of a primordial sense of meaninglessness and fear arise the Marlboro Man and the Cosmo Woman, but the erotic impulse turns against itself when sexuality is used in this way. It is a self-defeating and self-destructive sexuality which finds expression in the possession of one person by another rather than in the union of separate persons under the rule of God.

The current sexual revolution, as articulated in *Playboy* and *Penthouse* magazines, for example, actually represents an extreme form of sexual repression cleverly disguised behind slogans of freedom and liberation. The most significant thing to notice about these magazines is not the pornography but the association of pornography with promotional material of so many different kinds, including the cultural and political polemics found in the editorial pages. Criticisms of culture which focus upon such examples of pop pornography confuse the symptom with the disease. For it is the far more subtle and pervasive antagonism between the erotic and the mystical which results in the perversion of both dimensions of experience. The publishers of *Playboy* actually share with the preachers of the moral majority a similarly negative view of sex. Both groups focus upon the narrow question of gender and genitalia, *Playboy* advocating greater latitude in sexual behavior, the preachers prescribing greater restraints. Behind both reactions is a common tunnel vision which fails to recognize the basic unity of body and spirit. Behind the hedonist's gospel of free love and the repressive gospel of the moral majority lies a common preoccupation with the sex act itself.

Thus the central problem of American culture is neither materialism nor hedonism, neither moralism nor the self-righteous repression of the erotic; the central crisis of this culture is the stratification of the mystical and the erotic. The disembodied spirituality of popular religion is locked in a continual struggle against the dispirited hedonism of secular society. The resolution of this fateful struggle is not the triumph of the spirit over the body, but rather a rediscovery of the sacramental view of sex.

In this regard, I would measure progress, not by the latitude of behavior permitted in society, but rather by the degree to which the life of the senses is seen to be in symmetry with the life of the spirit. It is quite possible that a sexually and spiritually liberated culture would look quite conservative on the surface of things. Traditional values such as privacy and fidelity may find a rebirth in a truly erotic world. For, as the erotic is experienced as an all-pervasive impulse, people will be increasingly sensitive to the unity of consciousness itself. At the same time, religious experience will be deepened and enhanced as the material world is seen as a sanctuary of the spirit. Thus sexual fulfillment will be seen as an intrinsic element in salvation and the church will emerge as the erotic community per se. Already our religious communities function in a preliminary way as mediators between the erotic and the spiritual. In the churches and synagogues of America one finds an amazing array of human relationships. The primal roles of husband and wife, daughter and son, parent and child, lover and friend are acted out and extended beyond the narrow confines of the nuclear family. The most deeply personal dimensions of life are given public expression; the most profoundly physical experiences (from birth to death) are seen in their spiritual setting. When the organized religions function at their best, the whole of life is seen as being encompassed in the all-embracing love of God.

At the beginning of this century Sigmund Freud put forward the view that God was merely a reflection of the repressed memories of early childhood as the adult mind reached down into the depths of the unconscious for the materials from which to build a world more consistent with the deepest human hopes and dreams. While that description may be an accurate account of how God takes shape in the imagination, paradoxically the mirror image of this process may also be true. As the people experience a need to be reconciled with each other and the universe around them, the notion of a universal God of love may in fact be the most accurate and consistent expression of those same hopes and dreams. The fact that there is a symmetry between the experiences of early childhood and those of later life merely supports and confirms the biblical insight that there is a continuity in all creation. With Freud all theists would agree: belief in a just and loving God does fulfill the deepest, strongest, and most urgent human needs. With Freud many also agree: faith in such a God can be the product of neurotic and obsessive needs. Yet because faith is sometimes obsessive, one need not abandon the search for an authentic faith altogether. One must simply learn to distinguish at a deeper level between fantasy and reality. In fact, the descriptions of human consciousness which Freud constructed are completely consistent with the biblical notion of humanity as created in the image of God. Far from putting an end to faith, Freud inadvertently provided fresh support for a biblical view of creation and life transformed under the rule of Creator God.

3.
CHARLES DARWIN
The Origins of Doubt

One cannot begin to fathom the dilemma of western culture without reflecting upon Charles Darwin and *The Origin of Species*. Obviously, Darwin's theories about the evolution of life on this planet stand at the very center of the controversy between science and religion. We are reminded of this by the increasing efforts of creationists to gain equal time for the Bible in the public schools of America, but these rearguard efforts to turn back the pages of history and re-enact the Scopes trial are of far less significance than the continuing cold war between the world's leading scientists and theologians. For this is a controversy being conducted not in the rural countryside of Arkansas and Nebraska but in the leading universities and at the most advanced frontiers of human thought.

To be sure, the contradictions between evolution and the Bible have been addressed again and again. In fact, the critical issues were successfully resolved long before Darwin published his views on natural selection in 1859. What has not been repaired is the breach that opened up between science and religion generally in the period following the publication of *The Origin*.

Darwin realized that he had opened up the most serious problems at the interface of science and religion, but in the end he could not resolve them even to his own satisfaction. He ended his career in a state of total confusion about the one problem which his great book purports to solve; namely, how to explain the origin and evolution of life in scientific terms without an appeal to religion. As he confided in a letter to one of his closest colleagues, "I am in an utterly hopeless muddle."[1] Darwin's failure to resolve the problem of faith both personally and as a professional scientist has had a lasting effect upon scientific endeavor since the 1850s.

When Darwin set out on his epic voyage aboard the H. M. S. Beagle in 1831, he had no intention of rocking the world with controversy. At the beginning of his journey he was not a seasoned scientist well-equipped to address the fundamental issues of his time. He was a fresh graduate of Cambridge with a degree in theology. His personal agenda was to complete the requirements for ordination in the Church of England and secure a quiet, country parish where he could practice the ministry while at the same time pursue his favorite hobbies: hunting, fishing, and collecting rare specimens of rocks or beetles. His appointment as a "naturalist" on what was conceived as a routine scientific expedition to the southern coast of Tierra del Fuego would not yet have qualified Darwin as a professional scientist. The British Admiralty was not prepared to pay his salary; the government would only provide for his expenses and accommodations aboard the unwieldy and unseaworthy Beagle; but the chance to circumnavigate the globe and explore the coast of South America appealed to his sense of adventure.

The Beagle sailed on December 27, 1831, a date which Darwin later marked as the beginning of his "second life."[2] The notations in his diary and his letters home mark out the successive steps in the transformation from enthusiastic amateur to serious and dedicated man of science. To his father he wrote, "I think if I can so soon judge, I shall be able to do some original work in natural history. I find there is so little known about many of the tropical animals."[3]

At the beginning of the voyage his primary enthusiasm was for hunting, but after two years at sea he had given up his gun and had thrown himself entirely in the task of collecting specimens of rocks, plant life, and animals. Again he wrote home, "There is nothing like geology; the pleasure of the first day's partridge shooting or first day's hunting cannot be compared to finding a fine group of fossil bones, which tell their story of former times with almost a living tongue."[4] Already Darwin had exhibited a penchant for metaphor which, as we shall see, was central to his own thinking and characteristic of that whole mode of thought which today goes by the name of Darwinism.

If popular conceptions of the scientific endeavor call to mind technicians dressed in white robes in a laboratory somewhere, Darwin's journey aboard the Beagle gives us quite an alternative view. As the Beagle traced its course around the continent of South America, Darwin explored areas as diverse as the barren Falkland Islands, the tropical rain forest, the Rio Negro, and the volcanic mountains of Chile. On February 20, 1835, Darwin had one of those experiences that change the character of one's whole life work. While exploring the mountains near Valparaiso, his imagination was drawn to the solid masses of granite rising up out of the forests "as if they had been coeval with the very beginning of the world."[5] The granite fascinated him because it seemed to be the most basic and fundamental building block in the earth's solid crust. Penetrating to this basic, geological bedrock seemed to bring one close to the "classic ground" of creation.[6]

However, as he lay peacefully in a forest near Valdivia speculating about such impressions of nature, he felt the shock waves of a major earthquake. In the forest the drama of the earthquake was shocking enough, but when he returned to the port at Talcuhano he was horrified to find that every dwelling place had been demolished. The earth itself had been rent by deep crevasses, and the granite rock formations, which formerly appeared so solid and unshakable, had been shattered into fragments. "An earthquake like this at once destroys the oldest associations; the world, the very emblem of all that is solid, moves beneath our feet like a crust over a fluid; one second of time conveys to the mind a strange idea of insecurity, which hours of reflection would never create."[7]

As Darwin's awareness of nature broadened and deepened, so the solid crust of conventional scientific wisdom began to disintegrate. That all things are in a state of change and flux may have been the most important lesson which Darwin brought home from his long voyage. Darwin's notebooks give ample evidence of a mind itself going through a process of transformation. His imagination raced from one subject to the next. He did not focus upon any single issue of science; rather his thoughts ran free across the fields of geology, biology, paleontology, and anthropology. Curiously, in proportion as he became more deeply fascinated by science, Darwin became less interested in religion. He never seemed to experience a particular crisis of faith, but gradually and steadily his faith simply disappeared. He described the change much later in the pages of his *Autobiography;*

> I had gradually come, by this time, to see that the Old Testa-
> ment from its manifestly false history of the world, with the
> Tower of Babel, the rainbow as a sign, etc., etc., and from its
> attributing to God the feelings of a revengeful tyrant, was no
> more to be trusted than the sacred books of the Hindoos, or the
> beliefs of any barbarian. . . . I gradually came to disbelieve in
> Christianity as a divine revelation. . . . Thus disbelief crept over
> me at a very slow rate, but was at last complete.[8]

Such passages from Darwin, and there are many others of a similar nature, seem to offer to both defenders of faith and to devotees of secular science an obvious lesson. The moral drawn by both camps is that Darwin's life and work demonstrate the incompatibility of religion and science. Believers should avoid science because scientific inquiry inevitably conflicts with and possibly destroys religious faith; and, likewise, scientists should avoid religion because it has no more to do with the pursuit of truth than the "beliefs of any barbarian."

There seems to be a perfect syllogism here: true religion is undermined by science, and a true science is corrupted by religion; therefore, the two are locked in unceasing conflict. As tempting in its simplicity as this conclusion appears to be, and though this is precisely the lesson drawn out of Darwin by serious scientists and people of faith today, it simply cannot be sustained in the face of a deeper inquiry into his life and work.

To be sure, one must push to a level of analysis beyond that required in the acknowledgment that certain biblical stories, like the narrative of the tower of Babel, present a "manifestly false history of the world." If belief in God stands or falls on the historical accuracy of such stories, then the world's major religions would not have survived to Darwin's time. The question as to the truth or falsehood of religion, and its relevance to science, hinges on more basic issues than this, and Charles Darwin, drawing on his Cambridge theological education, was capable of wrestling with the issues at the deepest level.

When Darwin reflected upon the vast diversity of life as he saw it in the natural world and when he tried to understand how the various species came to be distributed in all their variety across the face of Europe and America, he quickly saw that the central issue was not so much a specific conflict between the affirmations of the Bible and the facts of natural history. Many leading scientists and theologians alike had recognized that the Bible could not be taken literally as providing an accurate or complete history of the natural world. The theory of evolution had been proposed long before Darwin's birth. In fact, his grandfather, Erasmus Darwin, had been one of evolution's leading exponents. Evolution had been widely debated in theological as well as in scientific circles, but until Darwin no one had demonstrated that evolution shed any more light upon the mysteries of life's origins than the reigning theory of that era.

In the opening decades of the nineteenth century the most widely accepted explanation for the diversity and distribution of life was the theory of special creation. According to this popular notion, all creatures great and small were the direct product of a special act of God. Whatever the sequence of timing, the place of origin, the pattern of migration, the growth or decline of populations, the crucial point was that each species was specifically created by God and uniquely adapted by the Creator for a particular setting in the natural world. A common corollary of this theory was that the species, as created by God, were immutable. Since God had designed each creature for a specific purpose at a particular time, any change in the characteristics of a species would be a perversion in God's plan of creation. In this view all life had been frozen in about the same form since creation. It is important to note that the theory of special creation is not exclusively the product of religion; it is not even rooted in the Bible. It was a conclusion supported as much by science as by religion.

Furthermore, special creation seemed to explain a great deal of what any good scientist saw in looking out upon the natural world. What any careful observer finds in nature is a vast array of animals all wonderfully adapted to their environments. Polar bears have thick fur capable of retaining body heat under conditions of extreme cold; fish have gills to draw oxygen from water just as lungs draw oxygen from the air. Likewise, birds have wings designed with awesome efficiency to carry them in graceful flight. Such observations, carried out rigorously and systematically, together with a careful analysis of animal behavior and anatomy, provided the underpinnings for the life sciences. All this early scientific work proceeded under the banner of special creation. The theory was both comprehensive and overarching; and it was thought to lie at the core of both science and religion, holding both together. The problem was that special creation had become a quick substitute for understanding. Darwin was the first to show that a systematic appeal to special creation as an all-encompassing dogma was incompatible with true science (just as, he went on to suggest, it was incompatible with religion).

For, once one affirms that a specific creature is a work of God, what more is there to learn? Having said all there is to be said about the ultimate origins of life, what interest remains to explore the finite questions, the detail that is required for a clearer understanding of why each creature has come to be or by what means the creator proceeds? Moreover, the theory of special creation tended to support the impression that each species was the result of divine fiat. An all-powerful God need not follow any prescribed laws; a particular species can be created by God completely without reference to any existing patterns or principles of nature. Were life in fact created in this way science would be quite literally impossible, for studying one creature or even one thousand creatures might tell one absolutely nothing about any other creatures. The secrets of life would be locked forever within the inscrutable mind of God.

Throughout his career Darwin's attacks upon special creation became continually more unrestrained. In the *Origin,* he chides those who affirm this theory:

> Do they really believe that at innumerable periods in the earth's history certain elemental atoms have been commanded suddenly to flash into living tissues? Do they believe that at each supposed act of creation one individual or many were produced? Were all the infinitely numerous kinds of animals and plants created as eggs or seed, or as full grown?[9]

Darwin clearly saw that special creation, taken as a total explanation for the origin of the species, was the fit subject of satire. Writing much later in *The Descent of Man* (1871), Darwin was totally unrestrained. Unless one is content to look at the phenomena of nature "like a savage," he argued, one "cannot any longer believe that man is the work of a separate act of creation."[10] Unfortunately, by the time he reached the degree of certainty required by his accusation that the proponents of special creation must think like savages, Darwin appears to have left behind him the major lesson of his own theological education. Also, in waging his battle against special creation he resorted to strategies of satire and derision which prevented him from taking his own theology much beyond where he had abandoned it to take up his adventures aboard the H. M. S. Beagle.

At Cambridge Darwin had read the work of William Paley who was the Church of England's most influential theologian. Paley was required reading at Cambridge and Darwin had to pass examinations on what were thought to be Paley's most important books, *Evidences of Christianity* and *Moral and Political Philosophy.* As an undergraduate Darwin approved so much of Paley that he went on to read *Natural Theology,* a work of more lasting significance and the one which made the deepest impression on him. At the core of Paley's theology is a clear and vivid analogy which makes his whole work seem deceptively simple. Paley's book begins:

> In crossing a heath, suppose I pitched my foot against a *stone,* and were asked how the stone came to be there; I might possibly

answer, that, for anything I knew to the contrary, it had lain there forever: nor would it perhaps be very easy to show the absurdity of this answer. But suppose I had found a *watch* upon the ground, and it should be inquired how the watch happened to be in that place; I should hardly think of the answer which I had before given, that, for anything I knew, the watch might have always been there. Yet why should not this answer serve for the watch as well as the stone?[11]

The reason, says Paley, is obvious. A simple examination of the watch leads the mind inexorably forward:

The inference, we think, is inevitable; that the watch must have had a maker; that there must have existed, at sometime, and at some place or other, an artificer or artificers, who formed it for the purpose which we find it actually to answer; who comprehended its construction, and designed its use.[12]

So, too, continues Paley, all the works of nature, indeed, "every organized natural body" whether plant or animal, simple or complex, likewise leads one inevitably to the conclusion that it too must have a maker.

For every indication of contrivance, every manifestation of design, which existed in the watch, exists in the works of nature; with the difference, on the side of nature, of being greater and more, and that in degree which exceeds all computation. I mean, that the contrivances of nature surpass the contrivances of art, in the complexity, subtilty, and curiosity of the mechanism; and still more, if possible, do they go beyond them in number and variety.[13]

Thus, Paley concludes, all the works of nature point to God in the same way that a simple machine points to its human maker. In this analogy Paley was repeating a formal argument which had been used many times before by philosophers and theologians, but he stated it in such a clear and convincing way that he gained a place in the history of ideas if only because his presentation was so lucid.

Yet there was more to commend Paley's book than its clarity. Paley argued not only as a theologian but also as a *scientist*. His text is generously salted with references to scientific literature of the period. He displays a familiarity with the latest findings in fields as disparate as biology and astronomy. Like Darwin, Paley's mind reached across the boundaries of every scientific discipline to draw the most comprehensive inferences and conclusions. Writing at the turn of the century, he even dealt in some depth with the latest theories of evolution as they had been developed a full decade before the birth of Charles Darwin (1809). Paley rejected evolution for precisely the same reason Darwin found these earlier theories to be unsatisfactory; that is, they could provide no real explanation how or why particular life forms emerged or what laws guided their development. Early theories of evolution could not provide a coherent explanation for the existence of birds as distinct from mammals, not to mention the larger challenge of accounting for the origin of the human species. Paley was justified in rejecting evolution in 1801 on purely scientific grounds; a great deal of research was needed before evolution could be raised as a comprehensive theory that would replace the notion of special creation.

One further point needs to be emphasized about Paley. His description of God's creative work in and through the natural world anticipates and successfully avoids the shortcomings of special creation, narrowly conceived. Paley argues that God's activity in the world does not consist in setting aside the laws of nature to impose a supernatural power and superior intelligence upon the mindless face of the material world. "When a particular purpose is to be effected, it is not by making a new law, nor by the suspension of the old ones, nor by making them wind, and bend, and yield to the occasion; (for nature with great steadiness adheres to and supports them;)."[14] But it is, according to Paley, by an activity "corresponding with these laws" that God works to create the wonders of nature. In fact, for Paley, God has sacrificed omnipotence, allowing the creative process to proceed according to clearly discernible laws of nature, and it is in and through the very laws of nature that God has accomplished the creation of life. "It is this," concludes Paley, "which constitutes the order and beauty of the universe. God, therefore, has been pleased to prescribe limits to his own power, and to work his ends within those limits. The general laws of matter have perhaps the nature of these limits."[15]

In fact, Paley's understanding of creation allows for the maximum element of continuity, uniformity, and regularity in nature. Far from setting up a wall against further scientific inquiry, Paley's natural theology represents an invitation and even a prelude to science, for under the rubric of his natural theology one may regard the phenomenon of nature with constant reference to the Creator. "The world thenceforth becomes a temple, and life itself one continued act of adoration."[16]

As indicated earlier, there lies an analogy at the heart of Paley's work, and for purposes of comparison the analogy can be represented graphically as follows:

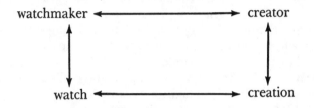

Paley put his analogy forward as a logically coercive proof for the existence of God, and, while his argument remains popular and appealing to many people even today, it has been attacked by philosophers of science and theologians so systematically and with such force that the impression is created that William Paley is completely passé. His four-sided analogy has been attacked from all sides by those who fail to see any justification for comparisons between a watch and a work of nature, between a watchmaker and God; it has been similarly asserted that one can learn nothing more about God from the study of creation than one could learn about a civilization which produced watches if one had no more evidence than an isolated mechanical device found by accident in a "heath" somewhere.

Indeed, the whole force of Paley's argument does rest upon his famous analogy, and he illustrates the first analogy with a second. Compare, he suggests, the human eye and the telescope. Both evidence similar principles of design and construction; both are modeled according to the same laws of optics; the eye differs only in being more versatile and more subtle in its operations. As the telescope is inconceivable apart from its designers, so too is the eye. In fact Paley argues that an examination of the eye is itself a cure for atheism. Thus *Natural Theology* consists of one analogy following after the next, and in the simple observation that this is so Paley's whole work has been written off as dead. For what is an analogy but an attempt to bring to light the hidden relationships between two or more dissimilar things? It is a bridge between two worlds, constructed of mere words. Surely, that is no proof of God!

As a proof, Paley's argument is rightly open to such criticism, for all analogies fall apart if you push them too far. However, Paley has been consigned to the footnotes of history far too readily by contemporary scholars. Today Paley is not only out of fashion, his *Natural Theology* is out of print. I believe this is a situation which should be corrected if only for the clarity which Paley brings to our understanding of Darwin, or, putting it the other way around, Darwin's misunderstanding and misreading of Paley needs to be accounted for because it is at precisely this point that Darwin's own theory falls apart.

Darwin thought that he had not only mastered Paley at Cambridge but also that he had defeated Paley in the formulation of his own concept of evolution. Hence he wrote in *The Autobiography*:

> The old argument of design in nature, as given by Paley, which formerly seemed to me so conclusive, fails, now that the law of natural selection has been discovered. We can no longer argue that, for instance, the beautiful hinge of a bivalve shell must have been made by an intelligent being, like the hinge of a door by man.[17]

Most contemporary scholars accept Darwin's words about Paley at face value. For example, historian Neal C. Gillespie drives another nail into the Paley casket in *Charles Darwin and the Problem of Creation*. "It has been generally agreed (then and since) that Darwin's doctrine of natural selection effectively demolished William Paley's classical design argument for the existence of God."[18] In fact, Gillespie is one of those secular interpreters of Darwin who goes to great lengths to reinforce the impression that the lesson to be drawn from Darwin is precisely that science and religion are completely unrelated and incompatible. "In the final analysis," he writes, "Darwin found God's relation to the world inexplicable; and a positive science, one that shut God out completely, was the only science that achieved intellectual coherence and moral acceptability."[19]

Gillespie convincingly argues that in order to transcend the limits of special creation it was easier to "shut God out completely." When a single theory so dominates the world of thought that further inquiry into basic questions becomes impossible, then certainly a case can be made for taking another look at the particular assumptions behind such a theory. However, if special creation had become such a debilitating dogma then, it certainly is not so now. In fact, when the best work of an important theologian like Paley can be dismissed in a phrase, as Gillespie has Darwin dismissing Paley ("Darwin downed Paley"[20]), then perhaps it is time to look through the wreckage of the old theory to see whether there are any useful elements that have been wantonly abandoned. In this case, a comparison of William Paley's natural theology with Darwin's own theory of natural selection reveals that Darwin did not defeat Paley after all; rather, he incorporated Paley into his own theory.

While denying that he could see the design that Paley saw in nature and loudly protesting the doctrine of special creation, he describes natural selection in such a way that the element of design in nature becomes all the more pronounced. While Darwin's theory is today put forward as a replacement for Paley, Darwin and Darwinism may be Paley's most important product. Yet the credits are denied not just to Paley, but more importantly to God.

If Paley's theology can be reduced to an analogy, all the more so can natural selection. The step-by-step process that Darwin went through in putting together his theory is well documented by friends and foes alike, and there is almost universal agreement as to what constitutes his basic building blocks. The most concise and at the same time accurate account of the origin of *The Origin* is contained in an essay by Stephen Jay Gould, who may be the leading disciple of Darwin today. Gould teaches biology at Harvard and his series of articles and books on natural history in itself constitutes an important milestone in the relationship between science and religion. More on Gould later, but first to his anatomy of natural selection. Always alert to the possibility that Charles Darwin is not the most perceptive interpreter of Darwin, Gould cites a note in what he calls Darwin's "misleading autobiography":

> In October 1838, that is, fifteen months after I had begun my systematic inquiry, I happened to read for amusement Malthus on Population, and being well prepared to appreciate the struggle for existence which everywhere goes on . . . it at once struck me that . . . I had at last got a theory by which to work.[21]

Gould draws upon his encyclopedic knowledge of the literature to demonstrate that Darwin did not stumble blindly upon Malthus. Rather, Darwin was intentionally rereading Malthus following an excursion into the distant fields of philosophy and economics. Just prior to his rereading of Malthus, he read a long review of philosopher Auguste Comte's *Cours de philosophie positive*. In this work Comte insists that any useful theory must be both predictive and, at least potentially, quantitative. Darwin then read a book on Adam Smith, the economist whose theory of society focuses upon the actions of the individual as the key element in a market economy. The work of a philosopher and an economist led Darwin next to a statistician, Adolphe Quetelet, who had applied a statistical analysis to the now famous and controversial claim of Malthus that the human population grows geometrically and food production only arithmetically, thus resulting in an inevitable and tragic "struggle for survival." Summarizing these intellectual wanderings, Gould writes:

> In reading Schweber's detailed account of the moments preceding Darwin's formulation of natural selection, I was particularly struck by the absence of deciding influence from his own field of biology. The immediate precipitators were a social scientist, an economist, and a statistician. If genius has any common denominator, I would propose breadth of interest and the ability to construct fruitful analogies between fields. In fact, I believe that the theory of natural selection should be viewed as an extended analogy—whether conscious or unconscious on Darwin's part I do not know—to the laissez faire economics of Adam Smith.[22]

Adam Smith's argument is the still familiar assertion used by those who favor an unrestrained, free-market economy. In order to achieve a productive economy providing maximum advantage and opportunity for all, individuals must pursue their private interests unrestrained by government or monopolies. Ironically, the maximum public good flows inevitably and naturally from the maximum pursuit of private profit. The theory of natural selection is nothing less and not much more than a simple analogy taken from the economics of Adam Smith and applied to the whole realm of living things. As individuals in the simple pursuit of their own private interests inadvertently strengthen the whole economic and social structure, so individual animals in their struggle for survival inadvertently work toward the betterment of a whole species.

In reading Malthus through the lens provided by Adam Smith, Darwin transformed Malthus from a prophet of doom into a prophet of evolution's unlimited promise. In so doing, Darwin drew still another analogy, this one from his own experience as a pigeon breeder. It is crucial to note that the very term "natural selection" refers to the activity of the breeding of domestic animals and is a precise analogy. As the pigeon breeder selects only those individuals showing the most desirable traits as most suitable for breeding, so nature selects those individuals best suited for survival, thus resulting in the slow but steady "improvement" of the whole animal kingdom. Note that Darwin's theory also took the form of a simple, four-sided analogy which may be depicted accordingly:

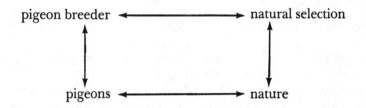

Thus Darwin proceeds from an analogy taken from the economics of Adam Smith to an analogy taken from his own experience as a pigeon breeder. The comparison with Paley is not limited to their penchant for analogies, for, when we make a specific comparison between the work of natural selection as described by Darwin and the work of God as described by Paley, the parallels are exact. Darwin depicts nature as a "power, acting during long ages and rigidly scrutinising the whole constitution, structure, and habits of each creature,—favoring the good and rejecting the bad."[23] Similarly Darwin writes:

> It may metaphorically be said that natural selection is daily and hourly scrutinising, throughout the world, the slightest variations; rejecting those that are bad, preserving and adding up all that are good; silently and insensibly working, *whenever and wherever opportunity offers*, at the improvement of each organic being.[24]

Darwin clearly states that there is a grand design in the silent and invisible work of natural selection. "We may look with some confidence to a secure future of great length. And as natural selection works solely by and for the good of each being, all corporeal and mental endowments will tend to progress toward perfection."[25] We remember that it was William Paley who was accused of being overly optimistic! In fact, when one summarizes all the things which Darwin has natural selection doing toward the creation and improvement of life on this planet, one has an exact duplicate of what Paley and theologians generally attribute to God. Thus if natural selection does everything that God is supposed to do, don't we simply have God by another name?

As conceived by Charles Darwin, the theory of natural selection shuttles back and forth between science and religion and does the work of both. In this context there is a further likeness between William Paley and Charles Darwin. Both worked at the interface of science and theology; they both developed and popularized powerful metaphors of creation. Both Paley's natural theology and Darwin's natural selection are basically creation myths much like the Gilgamesh epic or the stories of Genesis. They both give a clear and coherent account of the origins of human life that make it accessible to human understanding and invite further study.

For the same reasons Paley's analogies have been rejected as a proof of God, Darwin's could be rejected as science. Darwin was himself aware of this difficulty, and he commented:

> It has been said that I speak of natural selection as an active power or deity; but who objects to an author speaking of the attraction of gravity as ruling the movements of the planets? Everyone knows what is meant and implied by such metaphorical expressions; and they are almost necessary for brevity. So again it is difficult to avoid personifying the word Nature; but I mean by Nature, only the aggregate action and product of many natural laws, and by laws the sequence of events as ascertained by us. With a little familiarity such superficial objections will be forgotten.[26]

Yet we are in the grips of something more than a "superficial objection." Here Darwin is up against that fundamental problem of both science and theology; indeed it is the problem of cognition itself. In every science, including the science of theology, it is necessary to make generous and liberal use of analogies. In the pursuit of knowledge, analogies are the best we humans can come up with, for we only have a human way of speaking and a human way of understanding inhuman, superhuman, or subhuman things, and there is precious little that is human in this wide universe. We only occupy a tiny niche; we are the angels dancing on the head of a pin. As we look out upon the world and as we attempt to understand what is happening in a dimension beyond the immediate reach of our five senses, we have got to depict what is happening in human terms. Our analogies, our metaphors, and our anthropomorphic images are all that stand between ourselves and the external world. Darwin demurred briefly before this situation but tried to pass it off as a minor problem—"Everyone knows what is meant and implied by such metaphorical expressions"—but, of course, it is rather the case that no one knows what is meant by such metaphors. If the whys and wherefores of life on this planet could be included among the things everyone knows, then both science and theology would be superfluous.

Also, look what happens to natural selection when Darwin tries to get behind the analogy to a bedrock of fact which everyone can know. Behind his own images which personify nature Darwin asserts that "I mean by Nature, only the aggregate action and product of many natural laws, and by laws the sequence of events as ascertained by us." Hence there actually is no other basis or bedrock of fact behind his theories after all, except a sequence of events—*as ascertained by us*. Darwin, though, tried to do much more than give an accurate account of the sequence of events which we call natural history. He tried to give a scientific accounting of the precise relationship that exists between one event and another. Likewise, like a theologian, he tried to plumb the meaning of life's basic processes.

He maintained that natural selection, even as it represented an advance in science, also advanced our understanding of God. As he put it in the concluding sentences of the *Origin:*

> To my mind it accords better with what we know of the laws impressed on matter by the Creator, that the production and extinction of the past and present inhabitants of the world should have been due to secondary causes. . . . There is grandeur in this view of life, with its several powers, having been originally breathed by the Creator into a few forms or into one; and that, whilst this planet has gone cycling on according to the fixed law of gravity, from so simple a beginning endless forms most beautiful and most wonderful have been, and are being, evolved.[27]

Such positive and even rhapsodic passages are counterbalanced in Darwin by those comments inspired by the darker side of nature and natural selection. For, if natural selection works toward the improvement of every living being, nature moves each species forward with the inexorable force of extinction and death, eliminating by sudden violence, starvation, or any other of a thousand natural calamities all those unfit for survival.

Darwin tried to justify the element of waste and wanton destruction in the natural world in much the same way theologians try to reconcile the existence of evil and suffering with the existence of an all-powerful and all-loving God. He wrote in *Natural Selection:*

> We must regret that sentient beings should be exposed to so severe a struggle, but we should bear in mind that the survivors

are the most vigorous & healthy & can most enjoy life: the struggle seldom recurs with full severity during each generation: in many cases it is the eggs, or very young which perish: with the old there is no fear of the coming famine & no anticipation of death.[28]

One might ask, though, how Darwin could take the measure of an animal's joy or fear for the purposes of comparison. Darwin makes a bold attempt to bring suffering and death under the protection of evolution's all-embracing arms, but in the last analysis he meets with little more success than theologians who try to solve the problem of evil by talking of God's mysterious and inscrutable will. In Darwin's case the form of his argument is clearly that in nature's case the end justifies the means: "Thus, from the war of nature, from famine and death, the most exalted object which we are capable of conceiving, namely, the production of the higher animals, directly follows. There is grandeur in this view of life."[29]

Yet Darwin was aware that such "answers" are only partly satisfying and at times he pondered the possibility that there was no grand design in nature after all. Perhaps evolution moved forward haphazardly; perhaps even the highest forms of life, even humanity itself, are the product of blind chance. Shortly after the publication of *The Origin* he carried on a long correspondence with his friend and colleague, Asa Gray, confessing his own doubts and his sense of confusion about the end and ultimate directions of evolution.

I am conscious that I am in an utterly hopeless muddle. I cannot think that the world, as we see it, is the result of chance; and yet I cannot look at each separate thing as the result of Design.[30]

I am in thick mud; the orthodox would say in fetid abominable mud. I believe I am in much the same frame of mind as an old gorilla would be in if set to learn the first book of Euclid . . . yet I cannot keep out of the question.[31]

Darwin kept wavering throughout his lifetime. At one moment he would express confidence that natural selection represented nothing less than God's own design impressed upon the face of this whole creation, and in moments of doubt he could see neither the design in nature nor the evidence of God in creation. Evolution itself then amounted to nothing more than a random sequence of events strung together by fiat of the human mind. Darwin wandered between these possibilities throughout his life. He never succeeded in climbing his way out of his theological muddle.

Many disciples of Darwin have no such difficulty. Stephen Jay Gould, for example, is absolutely clear: God does not superintend natural selection. In fact, Gould extends himself again and again to say that evolution follows its own rules and heeds its own counsel; it cannot be the work of a divine Creator. By way of illustration, Gould argues in *The Panda's Thumb:*

> Our textbooks like to illustrate evolution with examples of optimal design—nearly perfect mimicry of a dead leaf by a butterfly or of a poisonous species by a palatable relative. But ideal design is a lousy argument for evolution, for it mimics the postulated action of an omnipotent creator. Odd arrangements and funny solutions are the proof of evolution—paths that a sensible God would never tread but that a natural process, constrained by history, follows perforce. No one understood this better than Darwin.[32]

Gould quotes Francois Jacob to the effect that nature is "an excellent tinkerer, not a divine artificer."[33] What his beguiling essay (and indeed his lifework in natural history) adds up to is the argument from design turned against itself. Gould tries to turn Paley upside down. The designs we see in nature resemble those of an amateur inventor, not an omnipotent Creator; parts originally fitted for one function are adapted to another; new species are "jury-rigged from a limited set of available components."[34] What Gould tries here, and elsewhere in his writing, is the most obvious and familiar maneuver of scientific atheism. He sets up God as a Perfect Being for the explicit purpose of showing how such a God could not possibly have created this imperfect world. In so doing he seems entirely oblivious to the lesson which "no one understood better than Darwin"; namely, William Paley's simple point that God, limited only by the laws of nature, must rely on artifice and contrivance. Whereas Paley rummaged the whole natural world for examples of God's design, Gould searches the same territory for those awkward, amateurish moves which show nature to be guided by something less than an omnipotent, omniscient Creator.

Gould writes eloquently, vividly, and graphically of natural selection; he uses one metaphor after another, but he assiduously avoids religious metaphors. In fact, he favors images drawn from the age of machines. He calls natural selection the "primary mechanism" of evolution. In another context, discussing human evolution, he writes "We are here for a reason after all, even though that reason lies in the mechanics of engineering rather than in the volition of a deity."[35] One wonders why it is more acceptable to see nature working like a machine. A machine is a human contrivance. To see evolution working like a machine does not solve the problem many scientists have seen in religion. If it is misleading to refer to creation as an act of God, it is doubly misleading to describe it as a machine. In making the transition from the former metaphor to the latter, one has only complicated matters, resorting to a more obscure form of anthropomorphic imagery.

The fact is we are locked into a position of having to describe inscrutable phenomena in terms accessible to human understanding. One can conceal this fact by resorting to abstractions or oblique images like Gould's, but one cannot thereby climb out of the muddle which is the human condition. All his disclaimers aside, Gould still describes natural selection as the creator, sustainer, and superintendent of life; as in Darwin, so in Gould, natural selection intervenes in nature to design and continually to redesign the diverse forms of life. Ironically, Gould proves Paley right: wherever we find design, there must be a designer; wherever one sees contrivance, one must conceive a contriver. For Gould and for many secular scientists natural selection functions as a stand in for God.

Could it be that Darwin with all his inconsistency and confusion was closer to the truth than Gould? Could it be that the most perceptive observers of nature draw their metaphors and spin their analogies freely from religious tradition as well as from the laws of mechanics, drawing upon the depths of imagination as well as technical reason?

In Darwin's age and in reaction against the stranglehold which the doctrine of special creation had upon the human imagination, it may have been necessary to construct a secular science, free of all appeals to God. In the closing decades of the twentieth century, however, when nature is not generally taken to be a window looking out upon divinity, it is an opportune moment to recapture something of the grandeur in this view of life. Nature is at once a sequence of events—*ascertained by science*—and an act of God. It may be time, in other words, to repair the breach that has opened up between the Darwins and the Paleys, to acknowledge that they were never that far apart, and to continue searching for a conception of the origin, end, and purpose of life that invites not only our continuing study but also our praise.

4.
KARL MARX
The Rise and Fall of Atheism as a Science

To most Americans the name Karl Marx is anathema. There would appear to be little reason for including him in a book that deals with either science or religion for, as everyone knows, his social theories were dogmatic rather than scientific and his atheism was notorious. Marx believed he had a theory that could solve the fundamental problems of humankind. Not only would he explain the human predicament without refuge to faith, but also a criticism of religion was to be the very first step in any real advance for humanity. Marx insisted that only after breaking the chains of superstition could the people of the world advance under the banner of a liberating science. In theory it did not matter whether people accepted this scenario, for Marx believed history would validate his far-reaching conclusions.

Marx predicted, among other things, that both organized religion and the nation state would wither away in the aftermath of a communist revolution. Today, however, the Soviet state, the first and foremost product of such a revolution, represents the most awesome concentration of political power on earth, and religion persists, perhaps even thrives, within the boundaries of the Soviet Socialist Republics. In the closing decades of the twentieth century we know that Marx's predictions for the most part have failed, yet more than half of the world's people live under the sway of governments that see Marxism as a source of almost mystical illumination.

In a year of revolution (1848) Karl Marx published his great *Manifesto of the Communist Party,* a call to arms addressed not only to the few actual communists of nineteenth-century Europe but also to the oppressed peoples of the whole world. Never mind that Marx's manifesto went practically unnoticed at the time; it stands today as a work which ranks with the most sacred books of any religion or the collected theories of any science. Marx begins with these foreboding words: "A spectre is haunting Europe – the spectre of Communism." In a few short strokes of the pen he goes on to define the exact nature of the communist threat, closing with a ringing call to arms:

> The Communists disdain to conceal their views and aims. They openly declare that their ends can be attained only by the forcible overthrow of all existing social conditions. Let the ruling class tremble at a Communistic revolution. The proletarians have nothing to lose but their chains. They have a world to win. WORKING MEN OF ALL COUNTRIES, UNITE![1]

While world revolution is already more than a century behind Marx's timetable, already the frontiers of revolution have swept far beyond the boundaries of Europe. The specter of communism today haunts Asia, Africa, and Latin America, and the confrontation between communists and anticommunists, always dangerous and violent, has become still more ominous now that the opposing forces are armed with nuclear missiles, submarines, bombers, and other engines of total destruction.

Ironically and tragically the continuous mobilization of communist and anticommunist forces all around the world has drained sufficient resources from the world economy as a whole to feed, clothe, house, educate, and put to work the entire populations of the Third World. Should the material resources that have been deployed to the military be redeployed to peaceful, economic development, the material promises of both communism and capitalism could be fulfilled. Hence the whole world is aware that the resolution of the present conflict is the number one problem for humankind.

For many people in Asia, Africa, or Latin America the questions addressed by Marxism are the most basic; before attaining precious liberties like freedom of speech or freedom of the press, the still more basic necessities of life must be secured— food to insure physical survival and simple justice so that the few do not continue to grow fat while millions starve. For most readers of this book, however, the questions addressed by Marxism are quite the reverse. Having secured the basic necessities of life, together with the freedom to use the vast resources of technology as a democratic people see fit, how can these resources be mobilized so that the pursuit of happiness may continue on a more equitable basis?

This was in fact the same problem Marx tried to solve, and he was convinced he had the answer not so much to the dilemma of the underdeveloped world but to the problems inherent in economies of affluence and overabundance. Contrary to the present situation in which communism is seen as a doctrine for the most deprived peoples in the most primitive economies, Marx designed his theories precisely to fit the circumstances found in the most advanced societies of Europe; namely, Germany, France, and England. He saw himself operating at the most advanced frontiers of human thought, pulling together the prodigious insights of German philosophy, French revolutionary politics, and English economics under the banner of an all-encompassing science. Marx believed he had found exactly the science that was needed to dispel the illusions of religion and so lead humanity forward from the immediate world of the here and now toward the twin goals of universal justice and universal benevolence. Marx intended to make the most devout prayers of millions of religious people into a down-to-earth program for social change. For the first time in history humanity could actually achieve in a communist society what was previously believed to be possible only in heaven. Thus, by turning the powers of the new science against religion, humankind could literally wrest ultimate power from God. One cannot begin to understand Marxism, its persistence, and its continuing power over the human imagination, even in the face of its obvious failures, without appreciating the genius involved in so successfully making science do the work of religion.

Ironically, an unflinching inquiry into the work of Marx provides exactly those diagnostic clues that may lead to a cure for the ills of western culture. Far from bringing an end to religion, Marxism may contain the secret to its renewal. For when Marx called religion the "opium of the people" he touched upon a truth that cuts to the heart of the human predicament. Marx's truth, however, is the obscured and half-forgotten truth of Old Testament prophets and New Testament Apostles, and it is the same truth which may set us free both from the specter of communism and from the ghostly specter of moribund religion.

In making this case, I will reflect not so much upon the polemical Marxism that one encounters in the revolutionary struggles being fought in Latin America or the theologies of revolution which these Latin American struggles have spawned; instead, I am drawing upon the original writings of Marx himself. I draw the reader's attention to Marx as his own ideas were taking shape so that one can more clearly see the crucial steps in the formulation of his "scientific atheism." It is this element in Marxism which most profoundly influences western culture as a whole. While Marxism today captures headlines as an obvious feature of revolutionary movements all across the Third World, of far gréater importance is the direct influence which Marxism has had upon the entire culture of the West.

Even as a militant Marxism provides the rationale for guerrilla war, Marx's particular brand of atheism has quietly but steadily advanced to the point that it is the de facto creed of scientists and technocrats all around the world. Without firing a shot or organizing a political party, the proponents of scientific atheism have already prevailed. Many of the assertions put forward by Marx in the middle of the nineteenth century are today the common assumptions of countless millions of people born and raised, educated and trained within the schools, colleges, and universities of the most advanced capitalist countries of the world. More surprising still, the chief mediators and messengers of Marxism have been the reigning theologians of the Protestant church. Only by learning atheism from Marx have these theologians managed to rescue theism from a premature death. In providing what he thought was the final criticism of religion, Marx laid the foundation for its reconstruction and renewal.

Marx had reached his negative conclusions about God long before he seriously studied either economics or politics. In fact, the roots of his atheism reach deep into his early childhood. Karl Marx was born in Trier, Germany (then Prussia) May 5, 1813, a descendant of Jewish rabbis on both sides of his family. His ancestry has been traced back in Trier to the seventeenth century and beyond Trier through a long succession of European rabbis and scholars as far back as the fifteenth century. Marx's father, Heschel-Heinrich Marx, rose without benefit of inherited wealth or social position to become the first Jewish lawyer in their predominately Catholic city. Karl's mother, née Henriette Presburg, was also a Jew, from Holland, and the granddaughter of a rabbi. As a child in Holland she did not experience the variety of anti-Semitism known elsewhere in Europe. The Protestant Dutch referred to the Jews as "sons of the old (Biblical) people" and as "our Jewish fellow Christians."[2]

Despite Heschel's success and Henriette's more fortunate experiences as a child in Holland, Prussia was entering a period of deepening anti-Semitism, with the government actively encouraging the conversion of its Jewish subjects to Christianity. On March 11, 1812, Friedrich Wilhelm III, King of Prussia, had issued a decree granting Jews limited rights of citizenship on condition that they adopt German surnames and conduct their business in German rather than in Hebrew or Yiddish. Full rights of citizenship, including the right to hold positions in government or to practice law, could be granted only upon proof of a Christian baptism. Orders went out from Berlin that local officials were to encourage such baptisms and give "all possible assistance" to anyone wishing to profess the Christian faith as a means of attaining the full rights of citizenship under the authority of God and King.[3]

In order to maintain his standing in the community and his livelihood as a lawyer, Heinrich Marx was baptized a Christian. Later, on September 13, 1824, the Prussian government issued another decree confirming a long-standing practice that non-Christians could not attend public schools. As Karl Marx was then six years old and of school age, he was baptized with his brothers and five sisters in the Trier Evangelical Church. The elementary school that Karl attended was directed by Johann Abraham Kupper, the same pastor who had prepared the family for baptism. Later, in secondary school, Marx attended compulsory religion classes for two hours every week. There too his teacher was the same Pastor Kupper.

Thus young Karl Marx was severed by baptism from a religion his family did not actively practice, and he was grafted into a new faith in response to a decree of the Prussian state. Little wonder that we find the more mature Marx expressing equal contempt for both Judaism and Christianity. In school he learned not to honor the religion of his ancestors but to despise it, and he learned as well that the most sacred ceremonies and practices of Christianity had become the mere instruments of an authoritarian state. To whatever degree Marx's negative assessment of religion was rooted in these early experiences, he soon found a mythological hero who presented exactly the model of rebellion he needed in facing the abusive authority of both church and state. As a doctoral student he turned to the study of late Greek philosophy and in the writing of his dissertation took up the work of Epicurus whom Marx called "the great enlightener." Epicurus, Marx asserted, well deserved the eulogy of Lucretius:

> When before the eyes of men, disgraceful life on earth
> Was bowed down by the burden of oppressive religion,
> Which extended its head from the high regions of heaven,
> And with gruesome grotesqueness frightfully threatened mankind,
> A Greek first ventured to raise his mortal eye
> Against the monster and boldly resisted it.
> Neither the fable of god, nor lightning or thunder of heaven,
> Scared him with their threat . . .
> Thus, as in reprisal, religion lies at our feet,
> Completely defeated,
> But, as for us, triumph raises us up to heaven.[4]

Furthermore, Marx identified with Prometheus, the Greek titan and rebel against the gods, as his personal role model. Marx's manifesto of militant atheism was written into the preface of his doctoral dissertation when he was only twenty-one. He applauded the creed of Prometheus: "In one round sentence, I hate all the gods."[5]

Later in life, when his own daughter asked him who was his greatest hero, Marx answered without hesitation, "Prometheus."

Throughout his career he read and reread the works of Aeschylus in Greek and thus kept his personal devotion to the Prometheus myth alive.[6]

In light of all this one might say that Marx's famous description of religion as the opium of the people was possibly the most charitable comment he ever made about faith and, at the same time, the most truthful. What did he mean? He did not mean what many students of Marxism have taken him to mean: that religion is a drug used by capitalists to keep a restless proletariat pacified. Religion does in fact function that way at times, as Marx often pointed out, but his famous aphorism occurs in the course of a much more penetrating analysis, and it reflects Marx's appreciation for both the power and the importance of religion. It was in the introduction to a major work on the political views of a philosopher, Georg Wilhelm Friedrich Hegel, that Marx put forward his Promethean faith as the one indispensable ingredient to a true understanding of both philosophy and politics.

> The *criticism of religion* is the premise of all criticism. . . . Religion is the general theory of this world, its encyclopedic compendium, its logic in popular form, its spiritual *point d'honneur*, its enthusiasm, its moral sanction, its solemn complement, its general basis of consolation and justification. . . . The struggle against religion is, therefore, indirectly a struggle against *that world* whose spiritual *aroma* is religion. *Religious* suffering is at the same time an *expression* of real suffering and a *protest* against real suffering. Religion is the sigh of the oppressed creature, the sentiment of a heartless world, and the soul of soulless conditions. It is the *opium* of the people. The abolition of religion as the *illusory* happiness of men, is a demand for their *real* happiness.[7]

Marx's greatest insight, which he arrived at in the course of reconstructing Hegel, was that all religion can be traced to its roots in the structures of society. Faith does not descend upon the world like a spirit from the heavens; it arises out of the experiences of real people as they struggle for survival in their particular life-situation. In this sense religion is "the encyclopedic compendium" of all human situations. All the suffering and the success of individual human beings, all their social relationships, are reflected in the symbols and images of their faith. Moreover, the specific character of religion is derived from what Marx called "the means of production." Since humanity stands above and apart from the whole animal kingdom by virtue of its capacity for making tools, machines, artifacts, ideas, and all the other products of civilization, in a very real sense it can be argued that humanity is what humanity makes. A given culture can be understood by looking at the ways and means by which property is owned and/or produced.

In this elemental insight Marx had found what he believed to be the basis for a new understanding of history itself. In fact, he argued that until his own theory was put forward history was largely an illusion. His was the first, true science of civilization. As his protégé and patron Friedrich Engels put it at Marx's graveside in 1883:

> Just as Darwin discovered the law of development of organic nature, so Marx discovered the law of development in human history: the simple fact hitherto concealed by an overgrowth of ideology, that mankind must first eat, drink, have shelter and clothing, before it can pursue politics, science, art, religion, etc; that therefore the production of the immediate material means of subsistence and consequently the degree of economic development attained by a given people ... form the foundation upon which the state institutions, the legal conceptions, art, and even the ideas on religion, of the people concerned have been evolved, and in the light of which they must, therefore, be explained, instead of *vice-versa*, as had hitherto been the case.[8]

Marx claimed that this view of history was thoroughly scientific. That is to say, he believed his theory reflected the actual situation of humanity rather than a mere fabrication of the imagination. His theory reflected extensive research into the realities of social life rather than mere superstition; it rested upon a solid foundation of fact rather than upon the blind authority of the Scriptures. As Marx applied his theory to the whole reach of history he saw a definite progression in the property relationships from which everything else in civilization flowed. He saw history moving from a period of primitive communism toward the fateful moment when private property was first introduced. Rather than living in aboriginal harmony, human beings soon began to compete for possession of cattle, for control of arable lands, and for natural resources as well as for artifacts and other products of human manufacture. With the increasing competition between various families, clans, and tribes the first violent conflicts, even wars, eventually proceeded.

As a consequence of the warfare, there was introduced a whole new era of history, the age of slaves. It was upon the foundation of slave labor that the whole of ancient civilization was erected. The great cultures of Greece and Rome, the dawn of the arts and sciences, the institutions of law and state, all these were made possible by the system of slavery. Over a period of several centuries the slave system was gradually replaced by medieval feudalism. There was a new organization of agriculture and craft using serfs rather than slaves, and a new class of workers, the artisans. Medieval cities also saw the development of a merchant class, independent traders, moneylenders, and, eventually, bankers. Slowly in the cities the guild masters and artisans began employing wage labor, and from this humble beginning the modern-day capitalist was eventually born. According to Marx, capitalism is characterized by the increasing division of all human society into two great, warring parties or classes, the bourgeoisie and the proletariat. From the throes of this class war the conditions for the final revolution in society are set; capitalism produces the seeds of its own destruction. In a very real sense Marx believed that capitalism would collapse of its own weight to be replaced by communism, history's final stage.

Obviously I am simplifying Marx's theory of history in all this. In doing so, I do not mean to underestimate Marx's contributions to our whole understanding of the past. To be sure, as a historian Marx received mixed reviews at best. Yet, it has been generally conceded that, since Marx, history cannot be written without a thorough appreciation of its roots in economics. In this respect, Marx's contribution is absolutely indispensable to our understanding not only of the past but also of the whole process of social change in which all peoples are presently immersed. At its best and in its subtlety Marxism ranks among the four or five great theories that have shaped our modern view of reality itself. As Freud was later to reveal the interconnecting tissue of human consciousness, Marx revealed the interconnecting structures, the skeletal shape, of all our social relationships. Yet Marx went beyond the historian's task of describing those relationships; he also played the part of a prophet trying to read the future from the story of the past, attempting to say what ought to be from what has been.

As we have seen, the cornerstone of Marx's theory is that everything else in culture follows as a result of changes in the means of production. As one economic system is replaced by its successor, class and family relationships, the legal system, and even religion are transformed accordingly. In all this religion does not play a passive role. On the contrary, it is employed by the ruling class as an ally in the war of resistance against change itself. It is crucial to understand the two-sided character of Marx's view of religion. In the first instance, he asserts that religion arises out of the economic and social conditions in which people find themselves. In situations of economic hardship and scarcity, people need an outlet for their feelings of helplessness and pain. "Religious suffering is at the same time an expression of real suffering and a protest against real suffering. Religion is the sigh of the oppressed creature." That, one might say, is the positive function of religion.

Yet Marx asserts that religion also and inevitably takes a negative turn. For, instead of offering real insights into the source of evil in the world, religion is used by the oppressor classes to conceal the actual situation and to wrap a veil of mystery around their own naked self-interest. Hence the real source of human suffering is obscured. What is this real source? For Marx, the ultimate source of evil in the world is the system of private property. It is from the accumulation of private property that all injustice flows, and it is against the evils of the property class that every effort of change must be directed. Unfortunately, at just this point Marx's whole theory of history collapses into a

Karl Marx   73

myth and Marx violates every standard that he himself believed
to be the basis of true science. In suggesting that Marx moved,
on the momentum of his own theory, from the realm of science
to the realm of myth, I am not speaking metaphorically. I am
simply recording the facts of the matter.

Marx's great work of economic and social criticism, *Das Kapital,* contains some of his most profound insights and also some
of his most serious errors. Here Marx deals directly with the
element of myth in both the Bible and contemporary capitalism,
but he also spins out some fanciful myths of his own. He traces
the development of modern forms of capital (or property) all
the way back to the beginnings of recorded history and in a few
short sentences summarizes the effect which the introduction of
private property has had upon the whole of human life. Marx
calls the first, rudimentary form of private wealth "primitive
accumulation" and he writes:

> This primitive accumulation plays in political economy about
> the same part as original sin in theology. Adam bit the apple,
> and thereupon sin fell on the human race. Its origin is supposed
> to be explained when it is told as an anecdote of the past. In
> times long gone by there were two sorts of people; one, the dil-
> igent, intelligent, and, above all, frugal élite; the other, lazy ras-
> cals, spending their substance, and more, in riotous living.

Actually Marx is confusing the story of the fall with the parable
of the prodigal son in his mixed metaphor from Scripture.

> The legend of theological original sin tells us certainly how man
> came to be condemned to eat his bread in the sweat of his brow;
> but the history of economic original sin reveals to us that there
> are people to whom this is by no means essential. Never mind!
> Thus it came to pass that the former sort accumulated wealth,
> and the latter sort had at last nothing to sell except their own
> skins. And from this original sin dates the poverty of the great
> majority that, despite all its labour, has up to now nothing to sell
> but itself, and the wealth of the few that increases constantly
> although they have long ceased to work. Such insipid childish-
> ness is every day preached to us in the defence of property.[9]

Marx is writing at several levels of irony here, and he is also
working at several layers of myth. His satire strikes out against

those hypocritical preachers of capitalism who use the story of the fall as the text for a sermon on the importance of hard work. Marx believed that such sermons were typical of Protestant preachers playing their role as court chaplain of the capitalist class. Marx had seen in his own youth how a state church could service the interests of the state, for evil as well as good. Having studied the Scriptures in secondary school, Marx was aware, of course, that neither the story of the fall nor the parable of the prodigal son were written as a device for keeping the working class happy in its servile position. Marx asserts that the Garden of Eden stories actually explain nothing; they merely echo the experience of a great majority of people who suffer and toil without finding real satisfaction. The Bible, according to Marx, tries to explain those experiences by transforming them into an "anecdote" about the past. The telling of such stories may be innocent enough but teaches us little about the driving forces of history. The myths of the Bible are not innocent, however, when they are used, as the capitalists use them, to conceal social and economic realities.

As indicated in the quotation just cited, Marx takes violent objection to those who see the factory worker as his own worst enemy. Marx rightly faults capitalists for seeing sloth not only as the original but also as the unpardonable sin. If anything qualifies as an original and fundamental sin, Marx asserts, it is the accumulation of private property. For it is this process which finally accounts for the vast discrepancy between the rich and the poor and the fateful tendency which Marx saw in nineteenth-century Europe for all wealth and power to be concentrated in the hands of a few, while many were driven deeper into poverty and destitution. It is, of course, tempting to jump upon Marx at this point for oversimplifying both the source and the nature of evil, but before looking into the limits of his theory it is important to see its strengths.

Marx's playful treatment of the Bible is revealing. When one tracks down all the biblical references in his writing, one discovers how deeply indebted Marx was to the sacred text of a religion he did not believe. One need not draw fanciful parallels between Marx and the Bible; one needs only to read *Das Kapital* with the Old Testament close at hand and the *Communist Manifesto* side-by-side with the New Testament. In fact, one can read Marx's work as constituting a running commentary on the Scriptures.

Among the more insightful passages in *Das Kapital* is the very first chapter on commodities. Here in section four Marx describes what he calls "the fetishism of commodities." By commodity Marx does not mean simply those natural commodities like iron ore or gold; he includes any product of human labor. Gold is a commodity, a product which can be bought and sold, precisely because human beings devote time and effort mining it. It is human labor and only labor which transforms a mere thing into a product. Labor is for Marx the source of all value; a commodity is simply a unit of human sweat and toil. Yet in the capitalist economies all commodities seem to take on a life of their own.

> A commodity appears, at first sight, a very trivial thing, and easily understood. Its analysis shows that it is, in reality, a very queer thing, abounding in metaphysical subtleties and theological niceties. . . . It is as clear as noon-day, that man, by his industry, changes the forms of the materials furnished by nature, in such a way as to make them useful to him. The form of wood, for instance, is altered by making a table out of it. Yet, for all that the table continues to be that common, every-day thing, wood. But, so soon as it steps forth as a commodity, it is changed into something transcendent. It not only stands with its feet on the ground, but, in relation to all other commodities, it stands on its head, and evolves out of its wooden brain grotesque ideas, far more wonderful than if it were to start dancing of its own accord.[10]

Hence all products of human manufacture take on what Marx called, a "mystical character." That is to say, human beings endow them with a value, even a life, of their own.

The whole of capitalist society is organized so as to produce more and more commodities, and the quantity, quality, and distribution of these products bears little or no relationship to their intrinsic value or to human need. At this point Marx draws the explicit connection to religion.

> In order, therefore, to find an analogy, we must have recourse to the mist-enveloped regions of the religious world. In that world the productions of the human brain appear as independent beings endowed with life, and entering into relation both with one another and the human race.[11]

One could not ask for a more exact parallel to the kind of writing found throughout the Old Testament. Marx might well have cited any one of several prophets of the Bible as authorities for his polemic on the fetishism of commodities. The Wisdom of Solomon (13:10) summarizes these prophetic warnings:

> But miserable, with their hopes set on dead things, are the men who give the name "gods" to the works of men's hands.

Clearly Marx was fighting against the same kind of idolatry that is public enemy number one within the world of biblical prophecy.

The parallels run consistently through the whole corpus of Marx and Engels. In *The German Ideology* (1845–46) Marx summarized this fateful error in human thought: "The phantoms of their brains have gained the mastery over them. They, the creators, have bowed down before their creatures."[12] Here Marx seems to be borrowing his phrasing directly from St. Paul who warned of the folly involved in confusing mere images of "mortal humanity" with the glory of "immortal God." As Paul looked out upon the human scene, the chief difficulty was that humanity had given up the truth for a lie, worshiping "the creature rather than the Creator" (Rom. 1:20–25). Of course, in Marx's version of this basic insight, the true creator is humanity, not God. Yet it is crucial to see that Marx's atheism leads him to many of the same conclusions that were made with equal force and clarity in the Scriptures.

As a parish minister writing from within the culture which Marx was describing, I can affirm his criticism as an insider. It is all too clear that capitalism does foster and promote an idolatry of exactly this kind. What we are up against here is not so much the misery of the poor as it is the pathos of the middle and upper classes. Having won their freedom from want or need, these groups sacrifice life itself in devotion to the mystical commodities of the American dream. Is this sin, though, the product of an economic system? The very same parallels between Marx and the Bible would suggest that the tendency of the creators to bow down before their creatures is rooted in something deeper than the system of private property. The temptation to worship a "phantom" of one's own brain is as ancient as human life itself. Thus, if Marx is exacting in his insights into the symptoms of human evil, he is not as close in the naming of its source. Simple exploitation of the weak by the powerful may be more deeply rooted than the particular economic circumstances of a given time. This tendency toward domination may have more to do with the forces that Darwin saw at work across the millennia than with the relatively minor changes from one system of production to the next.

Because Marx saw evil as rooted in a particular means of production, he could prophesy the end of evil as the inevitable result of a change in that economic system. Marx comes close to saying that if you do away with private property you also do away with evil. Revolution is thus a surefire method of redemption. Like the prophets of old, Marx looked forward in time to the collapse of the evil class and the vindication of evil's victims. With the violent overthrow of the capitalist system human life would be utterly transformed. Old animosities would seem suddenly unimportant; instead of struggling against each other in class war, people would now work together for the common good. Since the struggle to accumulate more and more property lies at the heart of all conflict, the abolition of property would allow people to relate once again to each other as human beings instead of as a means to an economic end. Equally important, since one's success in life would no longer be defined by the objects in one's possessions, people could once again take possession of themselves. The inner alienation between the mind and the body, the imagination and the senses, could be resolved, and a new transformed humanity would appear on the stage of history. The full creative capacities of the human species would now be addressed to the resolution of human needs, and work would become a question of personal fulfillment, a free expression of the best in human nature.

In communist society, Marx maintained, work itself becomes life's greatest pleasure:

> In communist society, where nobody has one exclusive sphere of activity but each can become accomplished in any branch he wishes, society regulates the general production and thus makes it possible for me to do one thing to-day and another to-morrow, to hunt in the morning, fish in the afternoon, rear cattle in the evening, criticize after dinner, just as I have a mind, without ever becoming hunter, fisherman, shepherd, or critic.[13]

This description of what might be called the typical day in the life of a communist worker sounds strangely like the ideal of the leisure class within the advanced industrial societies of the West, and the similarity is not entirely coincidental. For it must be remembered that Marx believed that a communist society would be erected on the shoulders of the most mighty industrial nations on earth. The first communists would inherit an economic machine of great technical and scientific efficiency, and these capitalist systems would become more efficient still once they could be utilized for the benefit of the whole people instead of just the few.

It is now obvious that Marx envisioned a complete transformation of human life by means of forces which could be seen at work in history, but in this hope he followed a biblical pattern as well—from the old alienation and conflict to a new life in freedom and justice; this same pilgrimage is charted out within the pages of the New Testament. In his letters to the Romans and the Corinthians Paul argues that, as sin and alienation have come into the world by "one man's trespass," so a new life in freedom will result from the action of "the one man Jesus Christ" (Rom. 5:12–21 and 1 Cor. 15:20–23).

Paul's summation of the whole of human history is this simple. "For as by a man came death, by a man has come also the resurrection of the dead. For as in Adam all die, so also in Christ shall all be made alive." Sentences such as these are today taken as proof positive that the Scriptures cannot be compatible with a modern, scientific understanding of the world. Yet Karl Marx, who has done as much as anyone to shape our modern scientific understanding, reduces history to an equally simple formula which one can paraphrase as follows: "As by one means of production came evil and exploitation, so by the abolition of that means of production will come new life for all."

For this reason, and reflecting these same parallels with the Scriptures, Marxism has been called "messianism without a messiah." Certainly Marx did not look forward to the coming of a savior, but he did cast the communist party in precisely that role. We see this most starkly in *The Communist Manifesto* where Marx simply asserts that the communists are prepared to lead the workers of the world in their revolution. He further asserts that these same communists could be trusted to advance the cause of the world's working people because they operate free of any sectarian or partisan interest. "They [the communists] have no interests separate and apart from those of the proletariat as a whole. They do not set up any sectarian principles of their own ... they always and everywhere represent the interests of the movement as a whole."[14] Marx has the communists operating on a plane of revolutionary zeal high above all the contradictions of history. Personal rivalries, partisan differences, disagreements between one nationality and another, all these symptoms of human fallibility and weakness can be overcome because the communists "have over the great mass of the proletariat the advantage of clearly understanding the line of march, the conditions, and the ultimate general results of the proletarian movement."[15]

What was this line of march which Marx so clearly saw? It was a linear march through the contradictions of history toward an ideal society, analogous in almost every respect to the religious idea of the kingdom of God on earth. Marx's "scientific" view of history can be compared, point by point, with the biblical view of history which Marx so vigorously rejected. In a simplified, outline form, one can construct a flow chart showing the fundamental stages in history as described in Marx and in the Bible:

Marx	*Bible*
Primitive Communism	Perfection in the Garden of Eden
Primitive Accumulation yields private property, exploitation, and war	The Fall yields original sin, suffering, and death
History of class conflict	History of conflict with God
The coming of Karl Marx and the Communist Party	The Messiah and the Early Church
War of Revolution	War of the Apocalypse
Dictatorship of the Proletariat	Thousand year Reign of the Messiah
Perfect Communism	The Kingdom of God

Because there are as many interpretations of Marx as there are of the Bible in circulation today, one cannot carry out such comparisons in exact detail. It is not necessary to establish that Marx was explicitly or consciously drawing upon the Bible. In fact, the deep irony of Marx was that in failing to see these very similarities between his own theories and the theology of the established church he also failed to see that his own movement was capable of repeating the most serious errors of established religion. As a movement, Marxism has gone through the same stages of growth and decline as did the early church.

We must remember that the communist movement which Marx was referring to in his *Manifesto* was, at the time of its writing (1848), little more than a small band of intellectuals uprooted from a particular country or political party. It operated largely in the realm of theory, far in advance of the actual revolutionary forces of the day. Historian James Billington describes this group of theoreticians perfectly as "the Early Church."

> The social revolutionaries who formed the Communist League in London were young, uprooted, and largely denationalized intellectuals. . . . The twenty-nine-year-old Marx could become a senior statesman in such a group. He was the prototypical displaced intellectual: a Berlin Hegelian who had discovered French social thought in Paris and then digested English economics during a second exile in Belgium. The "Communist Party" for which he purported to be speaking in his *Manifesto* existed only in his prophetic imagination. This "party" was a kind of *pied-à-terre* for a few intellectuals cut off from the main currents of European politics on the eve of revolution.[16]

Yet Marx puts forward this same group as the saving remnant that will transform the great class struggle into a liberating revolution. In so doing he places the communists in exactly the same position as the early Christian church, entrusted with the truth that would "set men free," the only difference being that in a perfect communist society there would be no need for God, since all human needs could be fulfilled through the science of world revolution.

As the past one hundred years have clearly demonstrated, the communist party makes a poor stand-in for the church of God. Rather than a society organized around principles of universal justice and universal benevolence, we see all power concentrated in the hands of a few party officials. Rather than the benevolence of an all-powerful deity, we see the deification of the very state machine that was supposed to have withered away. Instead of veiling the injustice of the world with theological talk about God's inscrutable will, we have seen the actual injustices of a Joseph Stalin or the Gang of Four, and the voice of protest is silenced by appeal to the inscrutable will of the party. Ironically, in putting itself forward as the saving remnant of humanity, the communist party has repeated all the evils of the established church, and in many instances the evils of communism have been far more extreme because the Soviet state has mastered instruments of destruction which the church in its most oppressive period never knew.

Marx's greatest error was in failing to see, within himself and his own movement, the same evils he saw so clearly in others, and because of this the communist party, especially in Soviet Russia, is a living contradiction of Marx's own insight. In an 1843 letter to his colleague Arnod Ruge, Marx defined the first requirement of his thought to be "*the relentless criticism of all existing conditions.*"[17] This was the first and foremost project which Marx was calling for as the necessary precondition to any real progress for humanity. This "criticism of all things" was to be the very first step that might ultimately lead toward "the building of the future and its consummation for all time." A heady ambition for a young man of only twenty-five! Yet even at twenty-five Marx had found the principle which is his most lasting contribution to the world; it is the same principle which could still redeem both Marxism and dogmatic religion alike.

The essence of Marx is the insight that any idea, any theory, any value, or any belief can be traced to its roots in society. Today doctrinaire Marxists follow this rule literally and often foolishly to look for the class interest in the most innocent situations. Hence the most insignificant novels and movies, the most inept decisions of government officials, and the most ill-conceived projects of private industry can be seen as phenomena of class war. Even so, there remains this essential truth of Marx, that many innocent-sounding ideas, plans, or projects do reflect the social position of their proponents. This is especially true, as Marx saw, of religious ideas. For example, feminist theologians have correctly pointed out that images of God as an all-powerful father quite clearly reflect the bias of the western church and its hierarchical male leadership.

Because the nuclear family has been organized under the authority of the father, it is not surprising that our concept of God has been organized around imagery of the all-powerful father God. As Marx realized, one can trace popular conceptions of God to their roots in social structure. To the extent that ideas of God are *merely* a reflection of the social conditions in which we all exist, a ruthless criticism of religion is called for. In this sense every believer must first become an atheist, for the greatest prophets and apostles have warned against substituting an image of mortal humanity for the glory of immortal God. Following Marx at exactly this point is of no less importance to faith itself than following the first commandment: "You shall have no other gods before me" (Exod. 20:3).

Marx's call for a criticism of all existing things suggests two points of departure for contemporary theology. First, one begins in full awareness that all human thought does in some degree reflect the life-situation of the thinker. Any concepts of God, any theological constructions, and any religious institutions are likely to reflect the finite interests of a particular people rather than the infinite truths of God. In fact, Karl Barth, himself a socialist and one of this century's leading theologians, took exactly this posture in his restatement of the Christian faith. His own criticism of all existing things led to a profound reaffirmation of God's transcendence and an equally profound skepticism about all claims for "natural theology." Barth picked up on Marx's insight that it is characteristic of organized religion to conceal the true dilemma of humanity and to obscure the injustices of a given society in a cloud of mystical illusion. Barth was as ruthless in his skepticism as Marx was, perhaps more so in that Barth systematically criticized all human ideas and institutions, especially institutional religion.

Barth, Bonhoeffer, and others have followed Marx in the conclusion that religion often is a mere reflection of the finite social interests of a particular group at a particular time in history. Hence, they argue, true fidelity to the God revealed in the Bible demands a clear decision for God and against all human stand-ins for God, even the established church. Speaking of the church, Barth wrote:

> Has it not always stood on the side of the "ruling class"? At any
> rate, has it not always been the surest guarantee of the existence
> and continuance of an order of classes which technically cannot
> be understood otherwise than as the order of superiority of the
> economically strong? And has it not with its doctrine of soul and
> body at least shown a culpable indifference towards the problem
> of matter, of bodily life, and therefore of contemporary eco-
> nomics? Has it not made a point of teaching the immortality of
> the soul instead of attesting to society, with its proclamation of
> the resurrection of the dead, that the judgment and promise

of God compass the whole man, and therefore cannot be affirmed and believed apart from material and economic reality,
or be denied or pushed aside as ideology in contrast to material
and economic reality?[18]

Yet in this same passage Barth also turns the corner on Marx,
reaffirming the positive function which even Marx had seen in
faith. For, if religion does reflect something real in human experience, then the truth claims of religion cannot be "pushed
aside" as false and illusory, over and against material and economic realities. Moreover, Barth recognized in the revolutionary
politics of Marxism a secular manifestation of the revolutionary
politics of God. Barth accepted and even embraced socialism as
a partial manifestation of the biblical hope for resurrection of
the dead. In the politics of revolution, he argued, "some part of
the resurrection of the flesh lies hidden."[19] Barth made explicit
the implicit parallels between biblical and Marxist views, arguing
that it was the truth of the Bible which had a prior claim if only
because the revolution promised in the Scriptures was more radical and more complete. Barth moved from the position of Marx
toward this century's most powerful affirmation of the majesty
and transcendence of God. His contribution to the reconstruction of biblical theism was the insistence that God cannot and
should not be identified with any human rule or ruler.

Barth's contemporary and rival among the theological giants
of the twentieth century, Paul Tillich, took off in a completely
different direction. Also a socialist and also convinced by Marx
that religion could function as a mask for the social bias of believers, Tillich took Marx's atheism one step further. Tillich saw
that even the idea of a transcendent God could be seen as a
product of the human imagination. Within this finite world of
time and space one cannot gain a certain hold upon the infinite.
What one can do is to take Marx's program for the criticism of
all social conditions as an invitation to theology. It is precisely
the task of the theologian to explore those points of reflection
where religion mirrors, as Marx said, the actual life-situation in
which people find themselves. If religion is "the general theory
of the world," if religion is the "encyclopedic compendium" of
all human experience, then what the world needs most is a self-

critical theology. Putting it another way, what Tillich found in Marx was the invitation to construct a theology of culture. One could follow the conflicts between the social classes, for example, to the point where those conflicts raised the ultimate questions of good and evil, life and death. Likewise, one could reflect upon the exact parallels between socialist politics and biblical prophecy and push through to a level of analysis deeper than Marxism has ever reached. When Tillich pursued theology in this way he found that culture offered a most fertile soil for theological inquiry. Tillich surveyed every realm of human culture and everywhere discovered signs and signals of God's presence. He moved from the position of Marx toward this century's most powerful affirmation of God's immanence and presence.

Thus Barth and Tillich became the leading theologians of the twentieth century. Both of them were indebted to Marx, though they followed Marx in radically different directions. Ironically, it was the "scientific atheism" of Marx which contributed most to their reconstruction of theology. In the final analysis the most important product of Marxism may be its impact upon Christian theology, for, if one can sustain the radical critique of culture which Marx called for, alongside the equally radical perspectives of the Bible, then one has the best possible opportunity for avoiding the mistakes of Marx as well as the mistakes of dogmatic theology. Reading Marx through the lens of the Scriptures we see how Marx fell victim to the very idolatry he so much feared in others. Lacking faith in God, he tried to make the communist party substitute as both Lord and Savior. Likewise, reading the history of religion through the lens of Marxism, we see the need for a more consistent Marxism than Marx himself sustained, and we find that the true fulfillment of scientific atheism is a more critical and creative faith.

Marx began his work completely convinced that the truths he put forward in the name of science would lead to the final defeat of faith in God. Now, more than one hundred years later, what his work truly reveals is the urgent need for a self-critical and reflective faith. For without such a faith science has lost its life-giving spirit, politics its final defense against fanaticism, and religion its humility before the majesty of God.

5.
PIERRE TEILHARD DE CHARDIN
Toward a Science Charged with Faith

Pierre Teilhard de Chardin (1881–1955) was the first, perhaps the only, leader of thought in this century to integrate pure scientific research with a religious vocation. At an early point in his career this paleontologist and Jesuit priest made it his personal mission to reconstruct the most basic Christian doctrines from the perspectives of science and, at the same time, to reconstruct science from the perspectives of faith. He would do this by overthrowing all the barriers that had been erected between science and religion in the past one hundred years. He would take the lessons learned from the study of nature as the foundation on which to reconstruct the Christian faith. He would single-handedly remake all the dogmas of his own Catholic Church, and he would at the same time remake the world of modern science on the model suggested by his personal experience of God.

Teilhard was seen in the Vatican as a threat to the integrity of the faith. Rome insisted that his religious writings should not be published; he was forbidden to teach or even to speak publicly on religious subjects; he was banished from his native country. Yet his ideas were disseminated informally and sometimes secretly by friends and colleagues in the church. He became a hero and a role model for a whole generation of younger priests and theologians. He set the stage for the renewal movements which finally came to flower in the era of Vatican II.

At the same time he also suggested a program for the reconstruction of science. He put forward a systematic critique of traditional science which was just as radical and just as provocative as his criticism of traditional religion, and he provoked equally extreme reactions in the scientific community. A small number of world-class scientists have taken his ideas seriously enough to structure their own work on Teilhard's model, but the majority of scientists have reacted as defensively as the Vatican theologians.

It is perhaps not surprising that our leading advocate of Darwinism, Stephen Jay Gould, has gone to work on Teilhard. Writing vehemently and dogmatically, like the guardian of an established religion, Gould asserts that Teilhard's whole enterprise is illegitimate: Teilhard's essential insights are incompatible with science. In addition to that, Gould has made it *his* personal mission to expose Teilhard as being guilty of the most outrageous scientific fraud of modern times.

Partly as a result of these defensive and dogmatic reactions to Teilhard, he is today tragically underestimated in both the religious and scientific communities. While many of his ideas have worked their way anonymously into currency and have been widely accepted, still Teilhard's innovative thinking has been taken seriously only by a minority of thinkers who see science and religion entering into a new era of cross-fertilization and creativity. For the vast majority, Teilhard's thought seems marginal at best, and his insights are not studied in the depth they deserve. This is partially explained by the active suppression of his ideas by the church and the suspicion of his ideas within the scientific community. Teilhard's obscurity is also to be explained, however, by his own style of writing and his tendency to wander into the realm of pure speculation. His fertile imagination sometimes led him into a fantasy world foreign to scientists and theologians alike. Yet even in the face of Teilhard's most serious mistakes I believe his initiatives should be pursued. When one cuts through his sometimes lurid prose, one encounters a series of highly imaginative and suggestive proposals for the reunion of research and religion. The questions raised by his work cannot be avoided. Anyone interested in extending the search for truth beyond the traditional frontiers of knowledge must wrestle with his basic affirmations.

Can science and religion be successfully remarried? Can a reunion of these old lovers infuse new vitality to the whole of western culture, as Teilhard passionately asserted it would, or, as his critics suggest, does Teilhard accomplish the reconciliation of science and religion at the expense of both partners to the marriage? Does he fatally compromise both sides in forcing an alliance which should never have been attempted in the first place?

It was at the heights of his career in paleontology while he was studying bones and fossils in northern China (in 1927) that Teilhard wrote what he called "a little book on piety" designed to convey both the sincerity and the orthodoxy of his faith to his superiors in Rome. In this book Teilhard speaks of *The Divine Milieu* and by its very title suggests his theme: the whole material world as the setting for a profound, mystical vision of God. It is in the world itself, as it is seen through the eyes of science, that the workings of God are most apparent. Teilhard's writing is graphic and unrestrained:

> All around us, to right and left, in front and behind, above and below, we have only to go a little beyond the frontier of sensible appearances in order to see the divine welling up and showing through. But it is not only close to us, in front of us, that the divine presence has revealed itself. It has sprung up universally, and we find ourselves so surrounded and transfixed by it, that there is no room left to fall down and adore it, even within ourselves.

> By means of all created things, without exception, the divine assails us, penetrates us and moulds us. We imagined it as distant and inaccessible, whereas in fact we live steeped in its burning layers. *In eo vivimus.* As Jacob said, awakening from his dream, the world, this palpable world, which we were wont to treat with the boredom and disrespect with which we habitually regard places with no sacred association for us, is in truth a holy place, and we did not know it. *Venite, adoremus.*[1]

Needless to say writing like this did not reassure the religious authorities in Rome, for Teilhard affirmed the material world as a source of mystical illumination. Though Teilhard did not directly criticize any specific doctrines of the church in his little book of piety, this work constitutes an assault upon the skeletal supports of traditional theology. Teilhard was just as provocative when he was trying to reassure as when he was trying to stir up debate. Early on, he describes his book in two sentences which were intended to convey the modesty of his position but in reality contained a theological time bomb:

> This little book does no more than recapitulate the eternal lesson of the Church in the words of a man who, because he believes himself to feel deeply in tune with his own times, has sought to teach how to see God everywhere, to see him in all that is most hidden, most solid, and most ultimate in the world. These pages put forward no more than a practical attitude—or, more exactly perhaps, a way of teaching how to see.[2]

Teilhard *says* that he intends no more than to "recapitulate the eternal lesson of the Church," but he goes on to assert that he is actually teaching the church how to see! As a scientist and an individual thinker, he is suggesting that the primary source of religious truth is to be found in the material world rather than in the *magisterium* of the church. In a real sense, it shall be science which shows theology how to see; it shall be the personal experience of a single priest which will indicate to the highest ecclesiastical authorities what is essential in Catholic teaching (as, by implication, he will show what is not essential).

As Karl Marx turned the world of philosophy upside down by revealing the foundations in society for every human theory, Teilhard tried to accomplish the even more difficult task of turning theology downside up. He tried to demonstrate that the material world, the world of rocks and trees, stars and planets, plants and animals, rather than being the neutral subject of scientific investigation, was in fact the soil from which would spring a new vision of the holy. The very subject matter of pure science was nothing less than a mirror in which one could see reflected the face of God. Hence Teilhard did not succeed in calming the anxious theologians at the Vatican, and they were rightly worried. He had raised the material world to a level of importance it had seldom held for theologians, Catholic or Protestant. In a more candid statement of faith written at the request of his confidant and colleague, Bruno de Solages, rector of the *Institut Catholique* in Toulouse, Teilhard put the issue on a personal, even confessional plane:

If, as the result of some interior revolution, I were to lose in succession my faith in Christ, my faith in a personal God, and my faith in spirit, I feel that I should continue *to believe* invincibly *in the world*. The world (its value, its infallibility and its goodness)—that, when all is said and done, is the first, the last, and the only thing in which I believe. It is by this faith that I live. And it is to this faith, I feel, that at the moment of death, rising above all doubts, I shall surrender myself.[3]

We must now ask what led Teilhard to believe so deeply in the world, or, putting it another way and reflecting the deep skepticism of our own era, what in the world is worthy of *belief* in the first place? For the vast majority of us, the material world provides the raw material for scientific research, not mystical illumination. Yet here is a professional scientist working at the frontiers of research, part of an international team of geologists, paleontologists, and anthropologists, and writing from an outpost of science in northern China, who boldly asserts:

If we Christians wish to *retain* in Christ the very qualities on which his power and our worship are based, we have no better way – no other way, even – of doing so than fully to accept the most modern concepts of evolution. . . . Surely the solution for which modern mankind is seeking must essentially be exactly the solution which I have come upon.[4]

One can easily see why Teilhard raised cries of alarm within the hierarchies of both the church and the academies.

Teilhard was born and reared in an eighteenth-century manor house located in the barony of Sarcenat near the provincial capital, Auvergne, France. The windows and terraces of the manor house look out upon the plain of Clermont, the rounded hillsides, and sleeping volcanoes that form the foothills of the Puy mountains. Growing up in a family of eleven children, Teilhard was reared in an atmosphere of discipline and devotion. In this highly structured family setting, Teilhard learned from his father, Emmanuel Teilhard de Chardin, the love of nature and natural history which later became so important to his spiritual life as well as to his science. The countryside was rich in rocks and minerals, animal life, and flowers, and Teilhard spent many hours with his father exploring, climbing the mountains, riding, fishing, hunting, and collecting outstanding examples of the local mineral, animal, and vegetable stock. Most of all he was attracted to the minerals, to the rocks, and to items of metal. He began a collection of shell casings and other metal objects. He seemed to be attracted to these objects because of their durability. He even called them his "idols." In his autobiography he records this memory of the earlier years:

> You should have seen me as in profound secrecy and silence I withdrew into the contemplation of my "God of Iron".... A God, note, of iron; and why iron? Because in all my childish experience there was nothing in the world harder, tougher, more durable than this wonderful substance.... But I can never forget the pathetic depths of a child's despair, when I realized one day that iron can be scratched and can rust.... I had to look elsewhere for substitutes that would console me.[5]

From that moment forward, Teilhard did not stop looking, searching, and exploring every corner and dimension of the natural world for his consolation.

Pierre's mother, Berthe Adele, seemed to have more immediate influence upon the child's religious life. "I was an affectionate child," he writes, "good, and even pious." Teilhard lovingly attributes to his mother, whom he referred to as "my dear, sainted maman," all that was "best in his soul." It was the influence of his mother which he looked upon to "rouse the fire into a blaze." The fire of which he speaks here is that of a mystical illumination from within. "And the spark by which my own universe ... was to succeed in centring itself on its own fullness, undoubtedly came through my mother."[6] Teilhard's life spins itself around these two poles of thought and feeling: his sense of fascination and wonder about the natural world and his sense of God's presence welling up from within the world. As he told the story much later:

> Throughout my whole life, during every moment I have lived, the world has gradually been taking on light and fire for me, until it has come to envelop me in one mass of luminosity, glowing from within.... The purple flush of matter fading imper-

ceptibly into the gold of spirit, to be lost finally in the
incandescence of a personal universe.[7]

At the age of twelve Pierre was sent as a boarder to the Jesuit
school of *Notre Dame de Mongre* at Villefranche. He was popular
among his peers and was eventually elected president of the
student body. He achieved a respectable academic record in religious studies and a superior record in science. At eighteen he
entered the Jesuit novitiate at Aix-en-Provence, and, when the
religious orders were expelled from France in 1902, he traveled
with the community to their refuge on the Isle of Jersey. While
studying with the Jesuits, he was introduced to the rigors of a
scholastic theology which he later so violently rejected, and he
had the opportunity to pursue his primary interest in geology
and the natural sciences. Physics, in particular, opened a new
dimension in his thinking. In the laws of physics he saw a verifiable basis for the unity that he had sensed in the natural world.
In this "world of electrons, waves, and ions" he felt "strangely at
home." The "mysterious" laws of motion and the electromag-
netic forces of the physical world seemed to suggest a secret,
"that at twenty-two," he vowed to himself, "I'd one day force."[8]

In 1905 Teilhard was sent to do his teaching internship at
the Jesuit college in Egypt and then in 1908 to England to finish
his theological training at Hastings in Sussex on England's
southeast coast. It was here that Teilhard's own thinking began
to develop in its full originality. Critical to his intellectual development was a reading of Henri Bergson's *Creative Evolution*,
which raised the theory of evolution to the level of a cornerstone
in a fully developed philosophical system. Teilhard found in
Bergson a theoretical basis for his personal feeling of intimacy
with nature and the material world. For Bergson saw a force at
work across the whole face of this planet as life evolved from the
most simple and original forms to the most complex. More important still, Bergson's work suggested to Teilhard that the
theory of evolution might be the precise theoretical tool that was
necessary to bring together the world of modern science and the
ancient teachings of the church.

Meanwhile Giuseppe Sarto was elevated to the papacy as Pius X. Both devout and reactionary, the new Pope was committed to lead Christ's church away from the corrupting influence of such "modernist" opinions. An elaborate spy system, complete with underground periodicals and secret codes, was devised in the process of seeking out and eventually bringing under discipline the church's errant, younger priests and scholars. The Pope set up committees of censorship in every diocese, and reports of heretical thought were sent directly to Rome. Catholic scholars and teachers were required to sign an anti-modernist loyalty oath.

Had Teilhard believed his primary calling to be a theologian, he might have seen in these developments a direct threat to his own future, but at Hastings his creative energy was moving still deeper into the realm of science. A chance meeting with the lawyer and amateur archaeologist Charles Dawson led to an association which was much later to present as great a threat to Teilhard's reputation as immediate events at the Vatican. At the time, though, Teilhard's association with Dawson contributed immensely to his progress within a scientific profession. Dawson introduced him to the prominent Arthur Smith Woodward, keeper of paleontology at the British Museum. Smith Woodward opened doors to the scientific establishment that would otherwise have been closed to the young Jesuit seminarian. In fact, Dawson and Smith Woodward were to become collaborators in one of the great events of paleontology, the "discovery" of the famous Piltdown Man, which they presented as an important missing link in the evolution of the human species. Teilhard participated with the two Englishmen in their excavations at Piltdown, and in the process his own standing as a promising young paleontologist was established in scientific circles far beyond the precincts of the church. When Teilhard left England to begin his doctoral work, he was to become a student and eventually a colleague of Marcellin Boule, the greatest physical anthropologist in France. Thus were the foundations laid for Teilhard's long and successful career as a paleontologist.

In 1953, however, Piltdown Man was exposed as a deliberate

hoax, perhaps the most astounding fraud in the history of modern science. Until recently Charles Dawson was believed to have acted alone in the Piltdown affair, but in August 1980, a quarter-century after Teilhard's death, Stephen Jay Gould put forward his own view that Teilhard was a coconspirator in the original fraud. Gould first published his accusations in *Natural History* magazine and has repeated his case with additional argument and discussion in a recent book, *Hen's Teeth and Horse's Toes.* Though his "evidence" is entirely circumstantial, Gould's accusations are tightly reasoned, as are the arguments of Teilhard's defenders who have written and published their own views in reply to Gould. The briefs for and against Teilhard are too complex to review here. Suffice it to say that the reconstruction of events that originally took place in the years 1908–1914 is difficult in itself. To draw firm conclusions based upon circumstantial references in letters and remembrances stretching across seventy years is almost impossible. Gould speculates wildly as to why Teilhard might have been drawn into the conspiracy. His tentative conclusion is that Teilhard thought he was involved in little more than a practical joke.

> Why not play a joke to see how far a gullible professional [Smith Woodward] could be taken? And what a wonderful joke for a Frenchman, for England at the time boasted no human fossils at all, while France, with Neanderthal and Cro-Magnon, stood proudly as the queen of anthropology. What an irresistible idea—to salt English soil with this preposterous combination of a human skull and an ape's jaw and see what the pros could make of it. But the joke quickly went sour.[9]

The great Smith Woodward took the forgery and unwittingly presented it as a major event in paleontology, but then World War I erupted and Dawson died in 1916, leaving, as Gould argues, Teilhard as the lonely keeper of the conspiracy. By war's end Teilhard was irrevocably committed to his own career as a paleontologist; he had seen his own mentor Marcellin Boule openly praise the Piltdown "discoveries." If he now confessed, his own future might be ruined. In these circumstances, what is a guilty coconspirator to do? Either he would confess his guilt and place his scientific career in jeopardy or he would keep silent on the whole subject and move on to build his career upon a more legitimate foundation.

In fact, Teilhard took a most implausible course of action were he in fact guilty as Gould has charged. In 1920 Teilhard published his own scholarly article on the Piltdown findings. Thus Gould would have us believe that Teilhard drew himself still more deeply into the web of lies, implicating himself far beyond the scope of a practical joke in a premeditated crime against the very scientific profession to which he was in the process of committing his life. Was the same man who made it his personal mission to show scientific endeavor to be a sacred calling capable of such duplicity? With such a serious potential for self-destruction? I doubt it.

The question which this entire episode raises in my own mind are *Gould's* motives in acting as accuser, prosecuting attorney, and presiding judge in the case of Teilhard vs. the truth. One suspects that there is more to Gould's motivation than a straightforward desire to solve a crime against science committed more than seventy years ago. Does Gould have an animus against Teilhard? Obviously he has, for Gould is a leading advocate of scientific atheism. Gould has made it *his* avowed intention to keep God, together with all superstition, racism, chauvinism, and other lies, out of science. Gould's books and articles argue eloquently for the integrity of science. Gould insists that real science can only operate with integrity if God remains shut out of it *completely*. In marking out the course of natural history one must look at the actual processes of nature, not impose upon nature any grand theory or design. Gould recounts horror story after horror story from the history of science showing how the preconceptions of scientists have meant in effect that their research was being put in service to a lie. He shows scientist after scientist fabricating results in support of the most pernicious superstition and simple prejudice. Gould is rightly concerned and angered by scientific creationists who lift his own words out of context to show that Darwinism is in a state of disarray or that the science of evolution is about to self-destruct.

Gould is so *rightly* angered by such false science and has suffered so many examples of religious superstition and stupidity that he can imagine no positive role for religion whatsoever. Since it has done and is still doing so much damage to science, it seems only prudent to separate science from religion completely. Given that conclusion, however, what does one do with the work of Teilhard de Chardin? Teilhard argues that the sciences of nature validate the fundamental affirmations of the Christian faith. While Gould is committed to shutting God out of science completely, Teilhard asserts that the only way to save science from self-destruction is to place God back in, at the very heart and center of the scientific endeavor. To scientists as well as to theologians Teilhard said, in words that hang fire, "Surely the solution for which modern mankind is seeking must essentially be exactly the solution which I have come upon."[10]

In a highly suggestive essay written in 1939, Teilhard traces the development of science from its earliest beginnings as a mere hobby to its present state as "the solemn, prime and vital occupation of man."[11] Teilhard follows science from its origins in the cultures of the ancient world through its period of expansiveness in the nineteenth century when it began to take on all the aspects of a substitute religion. Crucial in this period was the theory of evolution. Teilhard argues that the greatest single consequence of Darwinism was the "discovery of time."

> The perspectives of unbounded time with which we fill our lungs have become so natural that we forget how recently and at what cost they were conquered. And yet nothing is more certain: less than two hundred years ago, the world's leading thinkers did not imagine a past and would not have dared to promise themselves a future of more than six or eight thousand years. An incredibly short time; and what is even more disturbing to our minds, a span of simple repetition during which things were conserved or reintroduced on a single plane, and were always of the same kind.[12]

Teilhard points out that Darwin changed our understanding of time in much the same degree that Galileo transformed our sense of space. In both cases the boundaries of the universe were extended to infinity. As astronomy has exploded the geocentric

universe in which earth sits in its fixed place at the center of all
things, with the heavens above and hell below, so geology and
biology have pushed the horizons of time backwards into the
remote past and forwards into the far distant future. Also, as
life came to be seen as evolving across the millennia in a gradual
succession of living forms, suddenly a notion of *progress* was
born. With this new sense of moving forward in time from the
simplest life forms to the most complex, from the animal to
the human species, from the most basic colonies of bacteria to
the highest civilizations, science became much more than a
method of collecting and classifying the facts of life. Increasingly
science was seen as the specific means by which humanity would
move forward into the future. Teilhard writes:

> Henceforth science recognized itself as a means of extending
> and completing in man a world still incompletely formed. It as-
> sumed the shape and grandeur of a sacred duty. It became
> charged with futurity. In the great body, already coming to
> birth, of a humanity grouped by the act of discovery, a soul was
> at last released: a mysticism of discovery.[13]

In the nineteenth century science enjoyed such success at
explaining so many of the mysteries of life that it appeared to
many as if all the mystery could one day be explained away. In
physics one could penetrate to the heart of matter and develop
a clear understanding of that fundamental building block, the
atom. In biology, the evolution of life forms could ultimately be
explained through competition of the various species across vast
distances of time. By the same token, intelligence could be
understood as a function of the circuitry in the brain, and consciousness could be reduced to a complex series of chemical reactions, etc. In other words, argues Teilhard, the mysticism of
discovery was fast deteriorating into the mere "worship of matter."[14] The religious corollary of this trend was the death of God.
For, if all the important processes of life could be understood
through the tools of analysis just recently developed by science,
what further need remained for faith in God?

In Teilhard's view the situation has changed dramatically in
the twentieth century. In physics, the atoms themselves were

broken up and broken down into innumerable subparticles infinitely more mysterious than the alchemists ever imagined. In Teilhard's own words:

> The stuff of the universe, examined as a close texture, resolved itself into a mist in which reason could no longer possibly grasp, in what remained of phenomena, anything but the forms that it had itself imposed on them. In the final issue, mind found itself once again face to face with its own reflexion.[15]

Similarly, in biology, chemistry, and sociology the important phenomena could not be reduced to the simple mechanisms that were once thought to lie at the heart of all things. Far from continuing to explain away the remaining mysteries, science in this century has exposed still deeper mysteries at the very heart of matter itself. At a more mundane level science did not prove to be the unmitigated blessing it was once believed to be. Teilhard lived long enough to witness the explosion of the world's first atomic weapons, and with these weapons the fatal blow was delivered against the nineteenth-century idea of progress. If the science of Darwin, Marx, and Freud seemed to make certain the death of God, the nuclear arms race has secured the death of science as a substitute religion.

In reaction against a naive, anthropomorphic religion, science, in its century of triumph, had turned increasingly against any theory which cast nature into a human mold. Paradoxically, in this century, scientists have recognized that no clean line of demarcation can be drawn between the observer and the observed. The scientist, like the theologian, cannot take a completely "objective" position separate and apart from the phenomenon being studied. One inevitably sees the world through human eyes and conceives of the world in human images. Even when one makes every effort to avoid doing so, one still tends to make the world into a mirror.

A majority of scientists have dealt with this situation (as does Stephen Jay Gould) by opting for a militant skepticism. Not only has God been shut out of science but also any attempt to see in nature evidence of a final plan, purpose, or design is rejected out of hand. As Gould puts it succinctly in specific reference to Teilhard, "Perhaps the problem with all these visions . . . is our penchant for building comprehensive and all-encompassing systems in the first place. Maybe they just don't work."[16] This criticism completely misses the mark. Teilhard does not attempt to build an "all-encompassing system" and impose it upon nature. Teilhard looks to the natural world for signals of its *inherent* purpose, and he sharply criticizes Gould's brand of skepticism as narrow and debilitating. Writing much earlier than Gould, Teilhard anticipates his criticisms and answers his challenge:

> Asked whether life is *going anywhere* . . . nine biologists out of ten will today say no, even passionately. They will say: "It is abundantly clear to every eye that organic matter is in a state of continual metamorphosis, and even that this metamorphosis brings it with time towards more and more improbable forms. But what scale can we find to assess the absolute or even relative value of these fragile constructions? By what right, for instance, can we say that a mammal, even in the case of man, is more advanced, more perfect, than a bee or a rose? . . . we can no longer find any scientific grounds for preferring one of these laborious products of nature to another. They are different solutions—but each equivalent to the next. One spoke on the wheel is as good as any other; no one of the lines appears to lead anywhere in particular."
>
> Science in its development—and even, as I shall show, mankind in its march—is marking time at this moment, because men's minds are reluctant to recognise that evolution has a precise *orientation* and a privileged *axis*. Weakened by this fundamental doubt, the forces of research are scattered and there is no determination to build the earth.
>
> Leaving aside all anthropocentrism and anthropomorphism, I believe I can see a direction and a line of progress for life, a line and a direction which are in fact so well marked that I am convinced their reality will be universally admitted by the science of tomorrow.[17]

Teilhard asserts that nature is moving, erratically and haltingly perhaps, but nonetheless moving, towards higher and higher forms of consciousness. This movement is most apparent in the evolution of the human species. It is humanity in particular which has a clear concept of nature and nature's *inner* workings. Teilhard quotes Julian Huxley approvingly: humanity is *"nothing else than evolution become conscious of itself."* [18]

The specific insights that come into the foreground of awareness as one reflects upon the ascent of this species are both its uniqueness and its relatedness to the whole of the natural world. For Teilhard the most sublime product of evolution is the human person, the individual uniquely aware of itself as a person, yet also aware of its interdependence with the whole. Teilhard would agree with Gould to a point. One cannot talk scientifically about the superiority of the human race; one cannot separate the creation of humanity from the creation of other life forms. Humanity did not emerge by fiat of an all-powerful God. On the contrary, our origin and ascent follow the same path taken by all the creatures of the natural world. Human consciousness (including a consciousness of God) is the culmination of nature's own movement through time. Far from being imposed upon the formless face of the natural world, God emerges from nature as its final goal and purpose. Thus, science and religion are brought together in a direct, dialectical relationship. Teilhard states his argument most succinctly in the closing chapter of *The Phenomenon of Man*.

> To outward appearance, the modern world was born of an antireligious movement: man becoming self-sufficient and reason supplanting belief. Our generation and the two that preceded it have heard little of but talk of the conflict between science and faith; indeed it seemed at one moment a foregone conclusion that the former was destined to take the place of the latter. . . . After close on two centuries of passionate struggles, neither science nor faith has succeeded in discrediting its adversary. On the contrary, it becomes obvious that neither can develop normally without the other. And the reason is simple: the same life animates both. Neither in its impetus nor its achievements can science go to its limits without becoming tinged with mysticism and charged with faith. [19]

A science "tinged with mysticism and charged with faith." Are these words simply rhapsodic and metaphorical? Not for Teilhard. As a practicing scientist he saw the evolution of human personhood, not as an exception to the general rules of nature nor as a freak occurrence without relevance to other living things. He saw the "phenomenon of man" as an "arrow" pointing to the final goal and purpose of the universe itself.[20]

As science in this century has emphasized the interrelationship and interdependence of all things, religion affirms that the *unity* of all things is itself the most solid evidence of a God who embraces all. Growing from the same soil that has given rise to all other phenomena of life, human consciousness and the human personality appear to stand at the very top of the tree of life. If one were to project the forward edge of evolution into the future, especially as it falls increasingly under human direction and control, then it makes increasing sense to talk of a higher consciousness as being the inherent end and purpose of evolution. If evolution itself points toward a form of conscious life which has personality, perhaps God is the goal toward which this universe is moving after all. Hence the deep affinity which Teilhard felt between science and religion. "There is less difference than people think between research and adoration."[21] "Religion and science are the two conjugated faces or phases of one and the same act of complete knowledge."[22] Teilhard illustrates these concepts in the clean and simple image of the cone:[23]

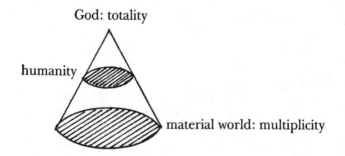

When human beings turn their powers of analysis upon the diversity and multiplicity of life (at the base of the cone), that is pure science. However, when humanity turns its powers of synthesis towards the summit, towards the totality and the future (at the pinnacle of the cone), that is theology. Yet science finds its fulfillment only as it turns from investigation and analysis towards synthesis: that is to say, seeing the totality of life and weighing its character, testing the relationship of the part to the whole. Likewise, those who engage in the search for God find their fulfillment only as they see the God who is available in the material world. A faith which is cut loose from the world is likely to be illusory and unreal. Conversely, the faith that truly counts is the faith which takes science as a fellow traveler in the final search for God.

In the past, Teilhard argues, theologians tended to see God as a supreme being standing over and apart from the material world. In this view God dwelt upon the high and remote plane of pure spirit, and therefore the way to salvation was to be lifted above the contradictions of the material realm onto a high spiritual plane. Teilhard writes, "Since Aristotle there have been almost continual attempts to construct 'models' of God on the lines of an outside Prime Mover."[24] The high and all-powerful God of traditional theology can influence the world only by intervening in its natural processes and contradicting its natural laws. In fact, many theologians delineate a crystal-clear line of demarcation between the natural and the supernatural. The chief signs of God's action in the world are taken to be those otherwise inexplicable events, apparently contradicting all reasonable explanation. Obviously this concept of God is still very much with us. In popular conception the most sure and certain sign of God's presence is to be found in those startling and unusual occurrences that seem to defy all understanding. A cancer victim suddenly goes into remission despite a clear indication from the medical authorities that death is imminent. The popular imagination has been trained through centuries of religious instruction to see God's appearance in the world as, by definition, a most un-natural and unusual event. Correspondingly, all hope for full and complete communion with God lies in the escape from the world which is possible only at death.

Thus one looks for a closer understanding of God by moving in a vertical dimension. One does not progress in life by moving forward in time but by escaping the contradictions of time and history in the eternal. It is precisely such a notion of salvation which has been seen as completely antithetical to science. A supernatural God can only be understood, in scientific terms, as arbitrary and capricious. It is not so much that scientists have locked God out of history; the breach has resulted as much from the sincere attempt of religious people to see God as perfect both in power and in love. Yet only a God who is removed from the ambiguities of life, as we know it, can be perfect. As Stephen Jay Gould rightly insists, such a perfect God could not have created an imperfect world. Such an act would have been completely out of character!

In the meantime, as theologians tended to define God more and more in terms of the supernatural, science has taken its stand in nature. In the years since Darwin scientists have seen human life evolving in a linear march through time. As the theologians defended God by building walls around the domain of the spirit, so science dug its trenches in the world of matter. Marx's dialectical materialism and his atheism are together the logical consequences of supernaturalism in religion. Scientific atheism is in fact the inevitable consequence of a theology which insists that knowledge of God must defy human understanding. When theologians insist that knowledge of God can only come through a miraculous act of divine revelation, rather than being discovered by reason, or that sinful humanity has no hope of salvation except by fiat of an all-powerful and all-loving God, then the dialogue between science and religion is interrupted prematurely. Moreover, religion has no role to play in a world which is committed finally and forever to science. That, Teilhard argues, is the greatest theological tragedy of our modern age.

Teilhard's modest proposal for the resolution of this dilemma is to chart a new course for both theology and science. If religion has seen its purpose as raising human life to higher consciousness in a vertical dimension and if science has seen its purpose in moving humanity forward on a horizontal plane within the boundaries of the material world, the obvious frontier of consciousness involves a movement both upwards and forwards. Again Teilhard offers a simple image to depict his agenda for the evolution of human consciousness.[25]

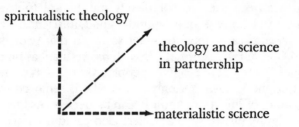

Teilhard's whole work can be considered as an open invitation. He extends an invitation to his fellow scientists, asking, imploring, cajoling them to consider both the theological assumptions hidden in their work and the theological consequences of their work. What is the *character* of the universe which emerges as reality is tested according to the scientific method? Conversely, what kind of God is consistent with the character of the world as it is seen through science?

Likewise, Teilhard extends an invitation to theologians and all people of faith, reasoning, exhorting, and provoking them to take the insights that come from science with a far greater degree of seriousness. In summary, he argues in an article written in 1939:

> In order to sustain and extend the huge, invincible and legitimate effort of research in which the vital weight of human activity is at present engaged, a faith, a mysticism is necessary. Whether it is a question of preserving the sacred hunger that impels man's efforts, or of giving him the altruism he needs for his increasingly indispensable collaboration with his fellows, religion is the soul biologically necessary for the future of science. Humanity is no longer imaginable without science. But no more is science possible without some religion to animate it.[26]

As Teilhard envisions the future, the greatest need is for a new type of seeker, or rather the rebirth of the original type once known to the world before the divorce of science from religion.

> This is a seeker who devotes himself, ultimately through love, to the labours of discovery. No longer a worshipper of the world but of something greater than the world, through and beyond the world in progress. Not the proud and cold Titan [Prometheus], but Jacob passionately wrestling with God.[27]

Thus, in the final analysis, Teilhard returns to the Bible and finds in the sacred Scriptures of his own tradition a God who is most compatible with a world in continual evolution. Not the static and unchanging God of the philosophers, the unmoved mover who stands over and against creation, but rather the same God who is so intimately related to the world as to enter into its deepest tragedies and struggles. The relevant texts of Scripture suggest that both the science and the theology of the future shall require not the detached and bespectacled observer but the passionate seeker who finds within the world of matter a supremely attractive center. The future of western culture may depend on whether enough of us have the courage to move with Teilhard from research towards adoration.

How does one evaluate Teilhard's diagnosis of the contemporary situation and his prescription for the future? Clearly his most controversial conclusion (that science finds its fulfillment in God) is not the product of logic and is not open to logical verification or falsification. It is in the nature of a character judgment about the cosmos. Teilhard devoted his life to exploring the mysteries of the material world, and he found that the world revealed a deep congruity with the character of the Christian God. Teilhard's daring affirmation that at the heart of all things one encounters "a supremely attractive center that has personality" can be taken in several degrees of seriousness. It can be taken lightly as an expression of enthusiasm for scientific research and of the feeling that the pursuit of truth in the natural world is analogous to the search for truth in the realm of the spirit. To the extent that Teilhard's work is treated as an expansive analogy, most scientists would resonate with his conclusions. At a deeper level, however, Teilhard is making an important observation about scientific endeavor and all serious searching for the truth.

Teilhard saw what is often ignored, forgotten, or repressed; namely, the element of faith which lies at the very heart of science. It is unlikely that anyone would become a scientist if there were not in nature some supremely attractive center and some assurance that scientific inquiry would lead one towards the truth. In setting out upon the adventure of science, one has to *believe* that the one who seeks will find. The health and vitality of science itself bespeaks of a universe which invites both our study and our adoration.

Yet many scientists balk at using the language of religion in defining their quest. Still more balk at Teilhard's identification of God as the goal and end of evolution. Like Gould, the majority of scientists *simply refuse to see* a distinction between a god who is arbitrarily inserted into science and a concept of God which grows organically out of science itself. Like Gould, the advocates of scientific atheism insist on taking the most crude and simplistic notions of God as representative. On that basis, neither Teilhard nor any theologian has a chance of being heard within the scientific establishment. Likewise, I am afraid to say, too few theologians are willing to enter into dialogue with science. While science is exploring vast new frontiers of understanding and has opened up entirely new vistas upon the world of nature, theologians have been reluctant to search for the fresh signs and signals of the Creator in creation. Therefore, our assessment of Teilhard cannot be complete at this writing. Teilhard can be evaluated fairly only by those who answer his invitation in the affirmative. Only as scientists listen to what is being said at the forward edge of faith and as theologians look into the world that is emerging under the scrutiny of science can true dialogue and deeper understanding prevail. The issue is far more important than the standing and reputation of Teilhard de Chardin. The real question is whether western culture can find its center and its sense of direction once more.

Shall the rallying cry at the forward edge of change be that of Prometheus, "I hate all gods!"; or shall we follow Jacob who found the courage not to defy but to wrestle with the God he found on the banks of the river Jabbok? Jacob wrestled and even fought with God until he emerged the morning after with a clearer sense of his own destiny, a better understanding of the world, and a closer relationship to his Creator.

6.
PAUL TILLICH
Theism Rewritten for an Age of Science

The theologian dies. His wife returns home and walks upstairs to his desk. Hannah Tillich describes what she discovered:

> I unlocked the drawers. All the girls' photos fell out, letters and poems, passionate appeal and disgust. Beside the drawers, which were supposed to contain his spiritual harvest, the books he had written and the unpublished manuscripts all lay in unprotected confusion. I was tempted to place between the sacred pages of his highly esteemed lifework those obscene signs of the real life that he had transformed into the gold of abstraction— King Midas of the spirit.[1]

Hannah Tillich's autobiography contains a brief, brutally honest account of the theologian's personal life. It portrays the Paulus she knew as husband and lover; it shows in concrete detail the situation of passion in which many of Tillich's ideas were conceived and nurtured. Like no other record in western literature, *From Time to Time* reveals what it was like to be life's companion to a titan of the spirit.

Reading this book, many would discount Tillich as a theologian. After all, why is a teacher in the church of God defiant of so many of the rules in conventional morality? Why the extramarital relationships, the *ménage à trois,* the experimentation with drugs, the Marxism, and, most remarkable of all, the development of a theological system that rests upon the premise that God does not exist!

When Hannah's book is read alongside all the other Tillich books and when the patterns of his whole life and work emerge from the immediate passions of their marriage, the answers to these questions become obvious. Hannah opened the desk containing Tillich's treasury of love letters nestled alongside his theological writings, and she has this fantasy. With a depth of conflicting emotion she imagines placing "between the sacred pages of his highly esteemed lifework those obscene signs of the real life that he had transformed into the gold of abstraction." These words *are* descriptive. It would not be far off the mark to say that Tillich did turn the deepest passions of life into the gold of abstraction. That is exactly what a theologian is supposed to do. The fire of religious feeling—faith and doubt, wonder, and awe—must be translated into an orderly pattern so that one may see and understand the fire's source. If one wants to learn from the religious experience of another person, one must have the instruments of thought necessary to discern what may be of value in a particular experience and what may not be of value.

Historically, the church has lost its way when its abstractions were no longer in touch with "real life" and no longer served a human need. Whenever the words of piety, sermons, or prayers are invoked in mindless repetition and whenever the words of the theologians no longer bear any relationship to the actual passions of a particular people, then it is time to mourn for the church of Christ.

One of Tillich's greatest contributions to theology, far greater than his mastery of abstraction, was his demonstration of exactly how deeply religious passion is rooted in human life itself. Tillich would have considered it a compliment to say that he succeeded in making the deepest thoughts and feelings accessible to understanding. Of course, Hannah's comment was not meant to be complimentary. She was referring to the tragedy of Midas, suggesting exactly what many of Tillich's theological opponents have charged: that he transformed life itself into an abstraction; that he turned the reality of God into the deadly gold of fanciful theory.

Thus, in the bitterness of her mourning Hannah imagines placing the love letters in between the pages of his theology, and, ironically, that act would have been appropriate. For, as Tillich struggled with the many loves and lovers in his life, he also struggled with the deepest and most imponderable love of all, the love of God. Tillich's most formidable work, the weighty, three volumes of his *Systematic Theology* could be described as a thoughtful record of one man's exploration into the depths of love. What Hannah says of the love letters can also be said of the theology. In the papers contained within Tillich's secret desk she could see "the many-colored flow of emotions he had aroused and that had aroused him—the red of passion, the sharp poisonous yellow of competition, the black of despair, the blue of devotion, and even the white of innocence he had not been able to destroy."[2] There were these and many other shades and hues of emotion represented in the letters and in the theology. For in his writings Tillich was able to discern the inner symmetry of the human spirit; he was able to explore the geography of human consciousness itself. In so doing he drew upon the newest of the life sciences, depth psychology. Almost single-handedly Tillich was able to separate the science of psychoanalysis from the atheism of its founder, Sigmund Freud, and to use its powerful tools of analysis in rebuilding the very faith which Freud so confidently assigned to oblivion. Though one may not find in Tillich a life one wants to emulate, one most certainly finds in his theology a number of insights indispensable to the renewal of religion in an age of science.

Paul Tillich was born on August 20, 1886, in a Lutheran parish house in Starzeddel, Germany. He was the firstborn son of Johannes and Mathilde Tillich. Writing to his parents about the infant, Johannes Tillich said, "Little Paul is still alive but his life is a continuous struggle with death."[3] The immediate threat to his life soon passed, but the theme struck in this early report was echoed again and again in the maturity of the theologian.

Johannes Tillich was a Lutheran pastor who eventually rose to a position of some power in the hierarchy of the Evangelical Church of Prussia. He was very much an authority figure for his son, yet there was a depth of love between them which was often felt if seldom expressed. Tillich also had a close relationship with his mother, Mathilde. She was strict and insistent, but the bonds of affection between mother and son grew stronger and stronger even as she fell victim to cancer in her early forties. Shortly before his mother's death he said to her, "I would like to marry you." Later Tillich summarized her influence: "My whole life was embedded in her. I couldn't imagine any other woman."[4]

Growing up in the parsonage, Tillich attended grammar school directly across the street from the church where his father was pastor. At home Tillich learned the meaning of the Christian holidays and seasons; in school he was instructed in the catechism, learned the great hymns of the church, and studied the Bible. In church he was exposed to the sacraments and other rituals of the Christian faith. As his biographers, Wilhelm and Marion Pauck, put it:

> In the center of the town stood the church; in the center of the year was the festival of Christmas; all else revolved around this place and this event. His feelings for the ecclesiastical and sacramental were for him part of the fabric of life from the very beginning.[5]

Yet Tillich's religious experiences were not limited to these traditional forms. When he was only eight, upon seeing the Baltic Sea for the first time, he felt the presence of the "infinite." This early experience was repeated and extended in both scope and depth throughout his life. As he writes in his short autobiography:

> The weeks and, later, months that I spent by the sea every year from the time I was eight were even more important for my life and work. The experience of the infinite bordering on the finite . . . supplied my imagination with a symbol that gave substance to my emotions and creativity to my thought. . . . Many of my ideas were conceived in the open and much of my writing done among trees or by the sea.[6]

Tillich reports that "all the great memories" of his life were interwoven with scenes from nature, with images of the landscape, with sea and soil, with the smell of the potato plant in autumn and the pine tree in spring. Yet at the same time Tillich was also fascinated by the city. "Visits to Berlin, where the railroad itself struck me as something half-mythical . . . developed in me an often over-powering longing for the big city."[7] It was in the city, first the cities of Germany, especially Frankfurt and Berlin, and later in America, especially New York, that Tillich was exposed to the cultural and social diversity that were as important to him as the solitudes and silences of nature. Throughout his life Tillich loved to travel from city to city and from countryside to countryside. He would travel alone or he would travel with Hannah. In fact it was their traveling which Hannah remembers as the cement of their often troubled marriage.

> Perhaps our moment came in our travels together. I was not only the listener for his geographical, historical, and philosophical-theological knowledge. I had studied art, I could show him lines, composition, color, technique, and the intuition of my own enthusiasm.... I could sense the flavor of past centuries, I could make the poems of the great and the faces of the kings come alive for him.[8]

As he was to cross so many borders and oceans during his life, so Tillich adopted "the boundary line" as an image which depicted and defined his stance in the world of thought. Throughout his career he found himself walking the narrow line between the temperament of his mother and his father, between the beauty of the countryside and the fascination of the city, between the church and secular culture, between politics and philosophy, between science and theology. In fact, his entire theological system begins with what Tillich called the "method of correlation." Tillich saw with stunning clarity the futility of a faith which provides answers to questions no one is asking; he saw the absolute necessity of making connections between the several dimensions of experience. While serving as an assistant minister in the Moabit, or workers' neighborhood of Berlin, Tillich found himself teaching a confirmation class. Trying to communicate the Christian faith to his students, he found the word "faith" itself to have little meaning and the meanings that still remained in such traditional vocabulary to be totally inadequate.

> This discovery determined his way of being a theologian: early in his process of development he cast his lot with the apologetic theologians, namely those who attempt to interpret the Christian faith by means of reasonable explanation. Tillich understood this to mean that one must learn "to defend oneself before an opponent with a *common criterion in view*."[9]

In his introduction to *Systematic Theology* Tillich notes that the apologetic theologian searches for the "common ground" beneath the feet of those who articulate the faith and those to whom faith would speak. He acknowledges the possibility that in seeking a common understanding with those outside the theological circle the theologian runs the risk of compromising faith. Yet the alternative approach suggested by "kerygmatic" theologians like Karl Barth is still less appealing. In Tillich's view one can no longer proclaim the faith, as it were, from a mountaintop. The Christian message cannot be "thrown like a stone"[10] at its target. Such an approach might seem acceptable to a theologian who can take refuge in the faith as though it were an impregnable fortress, but for Tillich no such refuge existed. Even within the relative serenity of the parsonage during his adolescence, he found that doubt about some of his father's deeply held beliefs could not be silenced. Fortunately, Tillich found a friend and confidant in Eric Harder, his father's assistant. The young minister not only listened to his questions but also accepted his doubts. Through the relationship with Harder Tillich realized that Christianity might not be wholly contained within his father's narrow orthodoxy. Also, during his years at secondary school Tillich began reading widely in philosophy, and as graduation approached he decided to pursue his questions about God one step further. In 1905 he registered at the University of Berlin, majoring in theology. Though he seriously considered following his father into the ministry, he also was drawn toward philosophy, a vocation which eventually led to his appointment as Professor of Philosophical Theology at New York's Union Theological Seminary in 1937.

Tillich's progress within the academic profession was interrupted, however, and his life turned completely around by World War I. Suddenly Tillich found himself headed toward the front, filled with nationalistic fervor and even enthusiasm over the opportunity to serve both God and country as a military chaplain. The realities of war changed all that. As Tillich put it years later, he and his compatriots in the military "shared the popular belief in a nice God who would make everything turn out for the best."[11] It became increasingly impossible to affirm the benevolence of God in the face of the horrors of trench warfare.

One of the duties of the chaplain was to bury the dead. As the violence of the war intensified, Tillich found himself spending more time digging graves than attending to his sacramental duties. In November 1916 he wrote to a friend noting his mounting sense of despair in the face of so much dying:

> I have constantly the most immediate and very strong feeling that I am no longer alive. Therefore I don't take life seriously. To find someone, to become joyful, to recognize God, all these things are things of life. But life itself is not dependable ground. It isn't only that *I* might die any day, but rather that everyone dies, *really* dies, you too,—and then the suffering of mankind. . . . not that I have childish fantasies of the death of the world, but rather that I am experiencing the actual death of this our time.[12]

More and more Tillich came to the realization that a certain God had died on the battlefields of Europe. The nice God who would make all things work out for the best had died. Tillich realized that the war had given concrete shape to the doubts of his adolescence. It was not only *his* doubts or *his* skepticism that prevented him from giving unqualified assent to God; but it was also the situation of total war which brought God universally into question. One could no longer easily preach about the benevolence of God or issue promises of peace from the heights of the mountaintop when the whole of western civilization seemed to be dying.

Did the war reveal the fatal flaws of capitalism? Was nationalism nothing less than the politics of death? Theological questions about the death of God were matched and mirrored by political questions about the self-destructiveness of nations and empires. Tillich began to see that his experience of God's absence was related to the experiences others were having, if in different form and context. Existentialist philosophy, Freudian psychology, and Marxist social theory explored the tragic depths of life and revealed the full force and power of the demonic. Doubt, death, and the demonic, three dark themes for Tillich, came to the forefront of his awareness during the war.

Still Tillich gained more from the war than the courage to trust his doubt. As a diversion from the terror of the battlefield, he and his friends would entertain themselves by studying picture-postcard reproductions of the world's great art works. For the first time Tillich began to *see* the importance of art. He found that he could escape the dread of the battlefield by contemplating the beauty of an expressionist painting, for example. The Expressionists did not merely reproduce the *surface* detail of objects of the world; houses, trees, and human beings were not for them what appears through the lens of a camera. Looking at an expressionist landscape one can see the inner light of things. One sees in their painting a dimension of *depth* lacking in realist paintings. Does the light one sees in such a painting have any relationship to the light that comes from God? Tillich found, as he kept looking at the paintings, that he was *doing* theology; he saw that in the dimension of their greatest depth all art and, in fact, all life evokes a religious response. Tillich reacted to the war and the politics of death by committing himself to be a theologian of life.

However, for a second time his course was altered radically and forever by an upheaval in his personal life. During the war his wife, Grethi Wever, had fallen in love with one of his closest friends. Having lost their first child in infancy, Grethi now announced that her affair with Richard Wegener had resulted in pregnancy. In June 1919 Grethi gave birth to her second child, whom Tillich named Wolf. Although Grethi soon left Tillich, she never married Wegener, and ironically the friendship between the two men survived both the betrayal and the subsequent divorce. More importantly, Tillich's reaction to the loss of his marriage was to plunge into what was to become a lifelong search for a new style of living, unfettered by what he increasingly saw as the chains of conventional morality. Tillich transformed his Berlin apartment into a "pension" for artists, writers, students, and others who were exploring the new possibilities of the "bohemian." Increasingly Tillich was drawn to the theater, to poetry and dance, to literature and every form of art. He would spend his free hours writing in a cafe and would gather around him friends, both male and female, who shared his interests in politics, psychoanalysis, philosophy, and the arts. The threads of these several interests were spun into the fabric of his lectures delivered at the University of Berlin, as well as his sermons and scholarly articles.

In January 1920 Tillich suffered the death of his sister Johanna. Ever since the passing of his mother Paul and Johanna had relied upon each other for the primal support and nurturing which can come only when siblings struggle through the stages of rivalry toward genuine intimacy. In February, as he still suffered with the depression which had followed Johanna's death, Tillich met Hannah Werner, an art teacher and poet, at a Mardi Gras costume party. In the weeks that followed they were plunged into a passionate, stormy affair which continued to deepen even though Hannah insisted upon carrying forward her plans to marry another man, Albert Gottschow. For two long years Hannah lived through the initial stages of a marriage that seemed doomed from the onset. Finally, after giving birth to a son (who soon died), she moved back to Berlin to join Tillich. Hannah and Paul were married in March 1924, but the ambivalence of their relationship continued and the struggle between them intensified. Fifty years before the idea of the "open marriage" provided the pretext for a best selling book of the same title, the Tillichs entered upon their marriage determined to defend their freedom in the face of all conventional notions of fidelity. In Tillich's view, keeping faith with another person had little to do with the exclusion of other relationships; the essence of fidelity was the ongoing commitment to a relationship of depth and passion. As long as one remained faithful to the depth of a relationship, what reason remained for the sacrifice of freedom? Thus in the 1920s the Tillichs worked out for themselves what they referred to as their "erotic solution."[13] Together they constructed a life in defiance of conventional morality. Together they set out to discover what the depths of love would reveal if their marriage were lived out without restraint against freedom. Though Hannah's book may not be a completely accurate record of their experience through forty years of marriage, still it is clear that in their marriage they shared both the depths of pain and the heights of ecstasy. Through the length and breadth of their relationship they did not cease to struggle with both the demonic and the divine, both the depths and the abyss of love (to use Tillich's abstractions in their exact context).

It is crucial to remember that this "experimental" marriage did not arise out of hedonism or self-indulgence. In a sense the marriage was consummated out of the tragedy of war and in the darkness of the shadow of death. As the nice and innocuous God of popular religion had died with so many millions of young men upon the battlefields of Europe, so the veil of respectability had been torn from the face of bourgeois morality. If the good Christian folk of Europe, Protestant and Catholic, could allow the entire continent to be ravaged by war, what value could be found in a popular morality which condemned the slightest aberrations in personal behavior, even as it tolerated and even justified the politics of total war?

When Tillich looked back upon the conditions leading to the war, he included in his diagnosis the exact problem I have been discussing in this book; namely, the tragic cleavage that divides the scientific from the theological. Tillich used one of the new psychological terms, calling it the "schizophrenic split in our collective consciousness." As he saw so clearly, the bewilderment and confusion of this age is rooted in the separation of science from religion, a condition which drives "the contemporary mind into irrational and compulsive affirmations or negations of religion."[14] In the period since Tillich's death it has become more and more apparent that the contemporary mind is also driven into compulsive affirmations or negations of science. As people see religion as a source of salvation *and* dangerous fanaticism, science is also seen as a source of lifesaving discoveries *and* the most terrible instruments of death. For Tillich, this situation required nothing less than a new understanding of God, a new theology which would take seriously the science of the last two hundred years.

Perhaps the primary reason that scientists and theologians have not engaged in more serious, productive conversation has been their shared misconception of God. From within the circle of faith and from without, religion is defined as an attempt to enter into relationship with a divine being. Hence the dialogue between science and religion is quickly aborted when theologians seem to be asserting the existence of something that science seems to deny; namely, an all-powerful, personal God. It is precisely this impasse that Tillich addresses throughout the length and breadth of his theology.

> It is just this idea of religion which makes any understanding of religion impossible. If you start with the question whether God does or does not exist, you can never reach Him; and if you assert that He does exist, you can reach Him even less than if you assert that he does not exist. A God whose existence or non-existence you can argue is a thing beside others within the universe of existing things. . . . It is regrettable that scientists believe that they have refuted religion when they rightly have shown that there is no evidence whatsoever for the assumption that such a being exists. Actually, they have not only not refuted religion, but they have done it a considerable service. They have forced it to reconsider and to restate the meaning of the tremendous word *God*. Unfortunately, many theologians make the same mistake. They begin their message with the assertion that there is a highest being called God, whose authoritative revelations they have received. They are more dangerous for religion than the so-called atheistic scientists. They take the first step on the road which inescapably leads to what is called atheism. Theologians who make of God a highest being who has given some people information about Himself, provoke inescapably the resistance of those who are told they must subject themselves to the authority of this information.[15]

So Tillich began what was the fundamental purpose of his theological endeavor: "to reconsider and to restate the meaning of the tremendous word *God*." In so doing he used his "method of correlation" to make the connections between questions that arise out of the life-situation of a particular people and the vast resources of the Christian tradition. If there were to be real communication between the scientist and the theologian, then Tillich must be able to identify a "common ground" between those two disciplines. Given his background and training in philosophy, it is perhaps not surprising that he concluded:

> The point of contact between scientific research and theology
> lies in the philosophical element of both.... Therefore, the
> question of the relation of theology to the special sciences
> merges into the question of the relation between theology and
> philosophy.[16]

Tillich argued that in every scientific theory there was an element of philosophy, as in every theology there is an implied philosophy.

For American readers the meaning of these assertions will be difficult to grasp. Tillich is speaking out of a philosophical tradition that has never taken root in America. For Tillich, philosophy appeared to be a bridge between science and religion, but, where Tillich saw a carefully constructed bridge, many readers of this book may find a gaping chasm. This may reflect one's lack of familiarity with German philosophy, but it must also be noted that the philosophical traditions in which Tillich stood have been subject to the same criticism as religion itself. For Tillich, philosophy was the study of those

> structures, categories, and concepts which are presupposed in
> the cognitive encounter with every realm of reality. From this
> point of view philosophy is by definition critical. It separates the
> multifarious materials of experience from those structures
> which make experience possible.[17]

Whereas science, in its ever-increasing powers of research, constantly expands the "multifarious materials" of human experience, philosophy attempts to illuminate the skeletal elements of consciousness itself. For Tillich, philosophy could function as the connecting link between science and theology because abstract thought had for him a direct relationship to experience. Tillich's abstractions were ontological and existential, but it is precisely the relationship to experience which has become so problematic today. Therefore, many readers of Tillich would conclude that Hannah was correct in her criticism. As a philosopher Tillich does appear to be a King Midas of the spirit, and the gold of his abstractions is a poor substitute for either the warmth of emotion or the burning clarity of the senses. Drawing upon his background in philosophy Tillich spoke of God as the

Ground of Being or alternatively as Being Itself. He spoke also of the Absolute and the Unconditioned, but today these terms are as problematic as a God who is conceptualized as a being existing alongside of all other beings.

Fortunately, however, Tillich had another way of defining the relationship of science and religion and therefore another solution to the "schizophrenic split in our collective consciousness." Tillich began his career in Germany but he ended it in the United States. Having been dismissed by the Nazis from his teaching post at the University of Frankfurt in 1933, he migrated to New York where he joined the faculty of Union Theological Seminary, continuing at that school for twenty-two years. Interpreting his ideas to an American audience, Tillich utilized the tools of analysis made available by depth psychology.

In his theories of the unconscious Sigmund Freud had brought to light a dimension of depth in human consciousness which the narrow rationalism of the nineteenth century had not allowed. In scientific terms Freud had achieved what Tillich described as "the emancipation of psychology from domination by physiology." Freud's great achievement was to defeat the notion that consciousness could be reduced to its physical underpinnings and then explained as a biological or chemical process.

> This discovery was important ethically and religiously particularly because it recognized—with questionable over-emphasis, to be sure—the fundamental importance of the erotic sphere for all aspects of the psychical life. It was an insight of which religion has ever been aware and which only the conventions of bourgeois society have relegated to the limbo of forgotten truth. . . . Speaking in the language of religion, psycho-analysis and the literature allied with it cast light upon the demonic background of life. But wherever the demonic appears there the question as to its correlate, the divine, will also be raised.[18]

While Freud insisted that his theories had discredited the truth claims of religion, Tillich saw that psychoanalysis actually confirmed many elements of religious tradition. Freud insisted that belief in God represented nothing more than the projection of images from the erotic experience of the infant into a supernatural realm, but Tillich drew the obvious parallels between that process and the biblical notion of idol worship and idolatry. He also turned Freud upside down when he suggested that, even when one sees that *every* idea and image of God is a projection, one must then follow the metaphor one step farther and notice that

> projection always is projection *on* something—a wall, a screen, another being, another realm. . . . The realm against which the divine images are projected is not itself a projection. It is the experienced ultimacy of being and meaning. It is the realm of ultimate concern.[19]

When Tillich writes metaphorically of the screen "against which the divine images are projected" he is certainly not referring to an object which exists like the screen in a movie theater. Tillich is not referring to something "out there." "It is the *experienced* ultimacy." One can always trace Tillich's most obscure abstractions back to the immediacy of human experience. That is why Tillich found such fertile soil in psychoanalytic theory. Freud had illuminated the pathways into the depths of human experience, and Tillich followed Freud's lead relentlessly; increasingly he spoke of religion as "the dimension of depth."

In a short but highly suggestive study of *Biblical Religion and the Search for Ultimate Reality,* first written as a series of lectures at the University of Virginia in 1952–53 and later published as a book, Tillich pulled together the philosophical and psychological elements in his thought to demonstrate that the truth claims of the Bible are in fact compatible with the deepest insights of science.

> If we enter the levels of personal existence which have been rediscovered by depth psychology, we encounter the past, the ancestors, the collective unconscious, the living substance in which all living beings participate. In our search for the "really real" we are driven from one level to another to a point where we cannot speak of level any more, where we must ask for that which is the ground of all levels, giving them their structure and their power of being.[20]

It is supremely ironic that while Freud thought he was driving God out of the sky, his theories in fact illuminate the very soil in which human experience of the holy is most deeply rooted and grounded. In Tillich's supple hands the tools of analysis supplied by Freud had been put in service to theology, and the same is true of the tools which Karl Marx provided. In fact, Freud and Marx performed much the same function within Tillich's theological system.

> Marxism can be understood as a method for unmasking hidden levels of reality. As such, it can be compared to psychoanalysis. Unmasking is painful and, in certain circumstances, destructive. Ancient Greek tragedy, e.g. the Oedipus myth, shows this clearly. Man defends himself against the revelation of his actual nature for as long as possible. Like Oedipus, he collapses when he sees himself without the ideologies that sweeten his life and prop up his self-consciousness. The passionate rejection of Marxism and psychoanalysis, which I have frequently encountered, is an attempt made by individuals to escape an unmasking that can conceivably destroy them. But without this painful process the ultimate meaning of the Christian gospel cannot be perceived.[21]

When Tillich writes of the violent and passionate reactions against Marxism, he is not merely speaking of a violence of emotion. During his final days in Germany, as Adolf Hitler began to exercise the dictatorial powers voted him by the *Reichstag* in March of 1933, Tillich saw his own study of Marxism, *The Socialist Decision,* first banned and then burned during a Nazi demonstration in the streets of Frankfurt. Hitler had manipulated the fear of communism and revolution from the left as a justification for his own revolution from the right. In burning Tillich's book, however, the Nazis were only demonstrating their utter disregard for the truth which could have saved them from the most terrible form of fanaticism, the fanaticism that comes from within. Tillich's book *was* radical in the true sense of that word; it pursued the dialectics of Marxism and the doctrines of Christianity to their roots. It raised the basic question as to why Marx had turned against religion at the same time as it addressed the similarly hostile reactions of religious people against Marxism. As he pursued these questions Tillich arrived at the somewhat surprising conclusion that this mutual hostility can be explained largely by the misunderstandings of science on both sides of the conflict. "The attitude of socialism toward religion could never have been as negative as it has become, if socialism had not thought that it had a substitute for religion at its disposal, namely, *science*."[22] Likewise, as Tillich demonstrates, the attitude of religious people toward socialism could never have been as hostile if the church had not accepted Marx's false premise that science is the deadly enemy of faith. Thus, behind and beneath the conflict between communism and Christianity stands the larger conflict over science. The tragedy which Tillich saw unfolding in Nazi Germany could be repeated in different shapes and sizes until and unless the original misunderstandings are unraveled.

In the years prior to World War II Tillich laid the theoretical foundations for what he called "belief-ful realism." He hoped that a dialogue between socialists and Christians could lead both to a politics filled with prophetic passion but without fanaticism and to a religion fueled by a hunger for justice but without the utopian idealism that would prevent it from ever being put into practice. Tillich looked forward to a new age "where the static opposition of socialism and religion would give way to a new synthesis characterized by economic justice and an awareness of the . . . divine in everything human."[23]

By contrast to this development, Tillich saw both capitalism and communism moving in a similar direction and making the same mistake. Both of them, in the name of science, have tended to exclude the element of the eternal in all things temporal. Describing this tendency in capitalist economies, Tillich writes:

> In the past man's relation to material things was hallowed by reverence and awe, by piety toward and gratitude for his possessions. In the precapitalist era there was something transcendent in man's relation to things. The thing, property, was a symbol of participation in a God-given world.[24]

By contrast, in the advanced stages of capitalism objects and possessions tend to lose their deeper, symbolic meaning. "They become utility wares, conditioned wholly by their utility . . . produced, treated and given away without love or a sense of their individuality."[25] Despite their differences both capitalism and communism have stripped away the religious meanings attached to material commodities and in the name of "scientific objectivity" have promoted an instrumental attitude toward the natural world. In this process capitalism tends to deteriorate into the merely competitive, the war of all against all, and communism into naked coercion. In both societies the mind of the mass prevails over the individual, and personhood is reduced to a series of numbers on the latest personality profile.

As Tillich followed Freud into the depths of human consciousness, exploring the sources of both the erotic and the demonic to the point where the question of the divine presented itself, so he followed Marx into the depths of social structures and societies, exploring the sources of evil and injustice to the point where the questions of justice are raised with prophetic passion. In other words, Tillich used the theories developed by Freud and Marx, exploring the mysteries of personal and social life, to the point where the theological implications began to be apparent. Following these atheists onto their own terrain and pursuing their paths of inquiry even deeper into the human predicament, Tillich was able to advance a new case for theism or, rather, a new theism framed in terms appropriate to an age of science. Tillich asserted that a critical, logical, and strictly scientific analysis of the human situation reveals "the presence of something unconditional within the self and the world"; or, putting it another way, "an awareness of the infinite is included in man's awareness of finitude."[26]

Does this line of reasoning constitute a new proof for the existence of God? Did Tillich discover a new argument for God spun out of the very theories that lie at the heart of scientific atheism? One can answer those questions in the affirmative only by using Tillich against Tillich. For he continually asserted that the existence of God is not open to argumentation. The existence of God is not something that can be proved or disproved. There are many direct statements to this effect in Tillich. For example, in the first volume of his *Systematic Theology* he writes:

> It would be a great victory for Christian apologetics if the words "God" and "existence" were very definitely separated except in

the paradox of God becoming manifest under the conditions of existence. . . . God does not exist. He is being-itself beyond essence and existence. Therefore, to argue that God exists is to deny him.

The method of arguing through to a conclusion also contradicts the idea of God. Every argument derives conclusions from something that is given about something that is sought. In arguments for the existence of God the world is given and God is sought. . . . But, if we derive God from the world, he cannot be that which transcends the world infinitely.[27]

It is the shortest sentence in this passage which stands out: "God does not exist"; but those words have a different meaning in context than they have out of context. Tillich asserts that existence is not an attribute one can use to qualify God. Tillich is not the atheist attempting to prove that there is no God, he is the fully committed theist trying to state in the sharpest and clearest possible way that God is "beyond essence and existence." Traditional arguments for the existence of God actually diminish God's importance by placing God alongside of and on a par with all other things, objects, persons, or beings. God does not exist in this narrow and limited sense. For emphasis alone, therefore, Tillich puts it in one round sentence. "God does not exist." In the sentence just preceding this, however, there is a gaping loophole, a giant exception. "God does not exist" follows hard upon this proviso: "*except* in the paradox of God becoming manifest under conditions of existence."[28]

Earlier in the same volume Tillich himself introduces the possibility that theologians may be able to prove not merely the existence of God but also the truthfulness of the entire Christian message. In defining his vocation, Tillich writes:

It is the task of apologetic theology to prove that the Christian claim also has validity from the point of view of those outside the theological circle. Apologetic theology must show that trends which are immanent in all religions and cultures move toward the Christian answer.[29]

If this were all one could get by way of a proof for God, it would be all one needs. While rejecting traditional arguments for the existence of God, Tillich introduces an argument of his own in the concept of "theonomous culture." As a theologian, Tillich saw it as his primary responsibility to point out the hidden religious dimensions in every realm of life. In art and architecture, in politics and economics, in psychology and sociology, in biology and physics, Tillich found confirmation of the Christian faith.

The Christian doctrine of the incarnation affirms that the divine has become manifest in human life. Applying this doctrine to the cultures of Europe and America and drawing upon his knowledge of civilization as a whole, Tillich tried to show that every cultural creation—a painting, a law, a political movement—has a religious meaning to be explored and a theological element to be explained. For Tillich the idea "secular culture" is a contradiction in terms, for even in a society which is militant in its atheism there is a hidden faith. Thus, as we have seen, the force of Marxism lies precisely in its success at becoming a substitute for religion, and the power of psychoanalysis is its rediscovery of the depth in human personality which is precisely the soil from which religion grows. Tillich summarized these conclusions in his famous aphorism, "Religion is the substance of culture, culture is the form of religion."[30]

Beyond this distinction between substance and form, Tillich had a more concrete image to express the relationship of religion to culture and especially to science. He spoke of science and religion as interpenetrating dimensions. Tillich saw in this image a solution to the serious problem raised by the metaphor of levels. For example, one way of distinguishing religion from science has been to say that religion deals with the soul and science with the body, religion with the spiritual and science with the material. However, it is this image which lies at the heart of our present conflict. For, as science explains more and more of human experience by its own tools of analysis, religion finds itself retreating onto a higher and higher level until it reaches such a great height that it no longer has any relevance to the basic processes of life. The decline of religion in the nineteenth and twentieth centuries has been the result of this multileveled analysis in which religion gradually recedes onto an ever more nebulous and remote plane of pure spirituality. By replacing the notion of hierarchical levels with the image of interpenetrating dimensions, Tillich was able to distinguish the scientific from the theological while still illuminating their close relationship. The separate dimensions move out in different directions, but they all meet around a common axis.[31]

Tillich's image of "the multidimensional unity of life"[32] sets the stage for his discussion of the most difficult problem at the interface of science and theology; namely, the tendency of science to define nature in terms of mechanical law and the insistence of religion that reality is, in its deepest dimension, personal. Christianity and all biblical religions are irrevocably committed to a personal God. Unless one can somehow bridge the gap that has opened up between the impersonal laws of nature and the personal God of biblical religion, the "schizophrenic split in our collective consciousness" will not and cannot be healed. Tillich addressed this problem directly in a paper written in reply to an address by Albert Einstein. The great physicist had spoken of the relationship of "Science, Philosophy, and Religion" at a conference on that topic held in September 1940 in New York City. Einstein identified God with the orderly laws of nature and he emphatically rejected the idea of a personal God. Einstein attacked the biblical notion of God from four sides. He asserted that the notion of a personal God is not essential for religion, that it is a mere superstition, that it is self-contradictory, and, most importantly, that it is incompatible with science.

Tillich's response to these arguments was published as chapter IX in his *Theology of Culture*. He answers Einstein point by point. Typically Tillich starts with a point of agreement. He immediately seeks the common ground on which a physicist and a theologian may begin. Certainly, he concedes, the concept of a supernatural being who intervenes in history and interferes with natural events is incompatible with science. If the universe were run by a deity who arbitrarily set aside the laws of nature, that not only would make a mockery of science but would also mean "the destruction of any meaningful idea of God."[33] Tillich insists that theologians must join with scientists in rejecting any notion that makes God into an independent cause of natural events, a natural object beside others or a being alongside other beings. "No criticism of this distorted idea of God can be sharp enough."[34] Then in characteristic fashion Tillich picks up Einstein's own terminology and tries to expose its deeper meaning. Einstein had spoken of "the grandeur of reason incarnate in existence, which, in its profoundest depths, is inaccessible to man."[35] This reference to a reality, provoking in humanity a sense of the holy while remaining beyond human understanding, Tillich identifies as "the first and basic element of any developed idea of God from the earliest Greek philosophers to present-day theology."[36] Tillich continues:

> The manifestation of this ground and abyss of being and meaning creates what modern theology calls "the experience of the numinous." . . . The same experience can occur, and occurs for the large majority of men, in connection with the impression some persons, historical or natural events, objects, words, pictures, tunes, dreams, etc. make on the human soul, creating the feeling of the holy. . . . In such experiences religion lives and tries to maintain the presence of, and community with, this divine depth of our existence. But since it is "inaccessible" to any objectifying concept it must be expressed in symbols. One of these symbols is Personal God.[37]

Repeating his earlier point, Tillich then admits that the symbolic character of the word *God* is not always realized and that the symbol is confused with some supernatural being which exists out there in an imaginary world of pure spirit. Thus, insists Tillich, the adjective "personal" can be applied to God only in a symbolic sense, as it is both affirmed and negated at the same time. "Without an element of 'atheism' no 'theism' can be maintained."[38] In what may be the shortest and most concise statement of his own theology, Tillich concludes his answer to Einstein:

> But why must the symbol of the personal be used at all? The answer can be given through a term used by Einstein himself:

the supra-personal. The depth of being cannot be symbolized by objects taken from a realm which is lower than the personal, from the realm of things or sub-personal living beings. The supra-personal is not an "It," or more exactly, it is a "He" as much as it is an "It," and it is above both of them. But if the "He" element is left out, the "It" element transforms the alleged supra-personal into a sub-personal, as usually happens in monism and pantheism. And such a neutral sub-personal cannot grasp the center of our personality; it can satisfy our aesthetic feeling or our intellectual needs, but it cannot convert our will, it cannot overcome our loneliness, anxiety, and despair. For as the philosopher Schelling says: "Only a person can heal a person." This is the reason that the symbol of the Personal God is indispensable for living religion.[39]

In the course of this argument Tillich refers to a physicist and a philosopher, even as he relates his argument to the experience provoked by pictures, tunes, or dreams. He affirms the multidimensional unity of life as an abstraction, and he ransacks the great diversity of life for the materials with which to build his theological system.

Did Tillich find evidence of divinity in so many places because he believed every dimension of reality intersected at some point with every other dimension, or did he arrive at his image of interpenetrating dimensions because he first experienced God in so many different arenas? It is impossible to say. Yet it is possible at this point to deny Hannah's criticism that Tillich transformed real life into the gold of abstraction in such a way that life was lost. Tillich's abstractions flowed out of his life experience and in turn fed back into life.

If there is a biblical character who typifies Paul Tillich, the strongest candidate is Abraham. For Abraham followed the call of a God he did not fully know toward a future he did not fully understand. Like Abraham, Tillich was uprooted from his native country and remained a pilgrim of the spirit throughout his life. Tillich was also uprooted from the conventions and even the faith of his own family. He also spent his days wandering from one place to another, exploring one experience after another, pursuing one relationship after another. He spoke of the multidimensional unity of life and in so doing he was able to demonstrate the relationship of science to religion, helping to heal the "schizophrenic split in our consciousness." This is not to say that every possibility Tillich pursued turned out to be productive. He experimented with the use of drugs but quickly concluded that drugs did not promote a deeper understanding of life's mysteries. He briefly became involved in politics in both Europe and America but did not find that partisan politics was his real vocation. Morally, intellectually, and spiritually he tried all things in order to enter into a deeper relationship with the Creator of all. He spared no effort in making God comprehensible in terms appropriate to an age of science. In fact, he turned the tools of science into instruments of theology. While he rejected the classical arguments for the existence of God, he demonstrated how the major questions raised by contemporary culture could lead one toward a fuller and deeper appreciation of the Christian faith. Tillich never claimed that he had discovered new proof for the existence of God, but he put forward such a persuasive case for Christianity that it surpasses all the old proofs put together.

7.
FRITJOF CAPRA *and* GARY ZUKAV
Where East Meets West

One could not ask for a more telling illustration of the impasse separating science from its roots in biblical religion than the two books, *The Tao of Physics,* by Fritjof Capra, and *The Dancing Wu Li Masters,* by Gary Zukav. They stand at the head of a whole catalog of publications linking the "new physics" and eastern mysticism. At this writing there are more than 280,000 copies of Zukav's book in print and over 380,000 of Capra's, and the publisher is planning an updated edition of *The Tao of Physics.* Clearly these authors have identified a strong, enduring interest in the linkages between science and religion; their books are classics in the whole field of antitraditional spirituality. In much of this literature the Judeo-Christian God is either ignored, satirized, or held up for ridicule as the antithesis of new wave sensibilities.

In the two books I shall examine here, numerous parallels are found between physics and eastern traditions—Hinduism or Buddhism, Taoism or Zen. Differences between physics and these traditions are glossed over so that the most sweeping conclusions are drawn. "New physics sounds very much like old eastern mysticism," writes Zukav,[1] and Capra outlines the identical theme:

> The purpose of this book is to explore this relationship between the concepts of modern physics and the basic ideas in the philosophical and religious traditions of the Far East. We shall see how the two foundations of twentieth-century physics—quantum theory and relativity theory—both force us to see the world very much in the way a Hindu, Buddhist, or Taoist sees it . . . physics leads us today to a world view which is essentially mystical.[2]

Both authors refer in passing to the mystical elements within the religions of the West, but this lead is not pursued. For both, biblical religion becomes a foil, a standard of bad faith, against which the stunning insights of the Einsteins and Heisenbergs can be compared and contrasted. At the same time, various ideas and fleeting impressions of mysticism are lifted out of context in wonderment and praise. Both Capra and Zukav succeed in their efforts to explain relativity and quantum mechanics in clear, arresting prose. (They both use very little technical language and almost no math.) Likewise, both writers show how suggestive and stimulating it can be to follow a lively imagination across the barriers separating different fields of thought. Yet these works are themselves the product of theological and biblical illiteracy.

There is not the slightest clue that either writer is aware of the major currents in western theology of the past one hundred years. Though world-class theologians have dealt with issues raised at the interface of science and religion and have discussed in some depth the very questions raised here, none of this scholarship is referred to in the text of either book, and there is very little in the footnotes or bibliographies of either writer to justify their wholly negative assessment of western religion. Both Capra and Zukav simply equate the Judeo-Christian God with the outmoded science of the seventeenth century, moving quickly to the conclusion that this same God has been surpassed by the latest science, just as the physics of the seventeenth century has been surpassed.

> The birth of modern science was preceded and accompanied by a development of philosophical thought which led to an extreme formulation of the spirit/matter dualism. This formulation appeared in the seventeenth century in the philosophy of René Descartes who based his view of nature on a fundamental division into two separate and independent realms: that of mind (*res cogitans*) and that of matter (*res extensa*). The "Cartesian" division allowed scientists to treat matter as dead and completely separate from themselves, and to see the material world as a multitude of different objects assembled into a huge machine. Such a mechanistic world view was held by Isaac Newton, who constructed his mechanics on its basis and made it the foundation of classical physics. From the second half of the seventeenth

to the end of the nineteenth century, the mechanistic Newtonian model of the universe dominated all scientific thought. It was paralleled by the image of a monarchical God who ruled the world from above by imposing his divine law on it. The fundamental laws of nature searched for by the scientists were thus seen as the laws of God, invariable and eternal, to which the world was subjected.[3]

This historical summary raises a host of questions which we will get to in a moment. For now, simply note that Gary Zukav draws the same sketch, showing how the philosophical, theological, and scientific theories of the West were integrated into the mechanistic model. In this view the universe is seen to be a Great Machine designed and assembled by God but now running on automatic pilot. As God stands above the world in perfect detachment, so the scientist must stand apart from nature to observe how the cogs and wheels of the cosmic mechanism really work. By way of illustration, Zukav describes Galileo's relentless effort to quantify and systematize the behavior of falling objects. Galileo saw that, whether one tries to understand the movement of the stars and planets in the heavens or apples and oranges falling from a tree, the important thing is to calculate their motions precisely. Galileo's work is exemplary of traditional science and Zukav draws out its implications:

> Once a relationship is discovered, like the rate of acceleration of a falling object, it matters not who drops the object, what object is dropped, or where the dropping takes place. The results are always the same. An experimenter in Italy gets the same results as a Russian experimenter who repeats the experiment a century later. The results are the same whether the experiment is done by a skeptic, a believer, or a curious bystander.

> Facts like these convinced philosophers that the physical universe goes unheedingly on its way, doing what it must, without regard for its inhabitants. For example, if we simultaneously drop two people from the same height, it is a verifiable (repeatable) fact that they both will hit the ground at the same time, regardless of their weights. We can measure their fall, acceleration, and impact the same way that we measure the fall, acceleration, and impact of stones. In fact, the results will be the

same as if they *were* stones. . . . The feelings of our subjects matter not in the least. When we take them up the tower again (struggling this time) and drop them off again, they fall with the same acceleration and duration that they did the first time, even though now, of course, they are both fighting mad. The Great Machine is impersonal. In fact, it was precisely this impersonality that inspired scientists to strive for "absolute objectivity."[4]

As Zukav and Capra remind us, however, the new physics reveals absolute objectivity to be impossible. In subatomic physics one cannot take a measurement without changing the particle one seeks to measure, so there is a degree of uncertainty in all calculations at the microscopic level. More importantly, one cannot prove that the material world exists apart from our observations of it. In this century physics has tended to move away from a mechanistic model of the universe toward an organic model. Now it is widely recognized that even the most objective scientist is very much part of nature. We change the world as we seek to understand it and, in understanding it, the world changes us. No one is in a position to stand over and apart from the world so as to see the truth, the whole truth, and nothing but the truth. In fact, the question arises whether there is any truth apart from our perceptions.

Zukav and Capra both outline the implications of relativity and quantum mechanics, bringing us back to the point of departure taken in chapter 1 of this book. Rather than seeing the moon rock as part of some sure and certain reality existing out there beyond the fleeting moods and emotions of the human mind, we now see objective and subjective, material and mental realms to be inseparable. In this view we are taken beyond the perception that all our mental life has a basis in the chemical and electrical circuitry of the brain. We are led to the more surprising possibility that the whole universe must be taken into account as one tries to understand the shape and structure of consciousness itself. Rather than seeing the brain as the locus of conscious life, with a solid line of demarcation drawn between the inner world of thought and the outer world of things, the new physics suggests that both inner and outer worlds are inseparable parts of a unified whole. Some physicists even speak of various particles as possessing properties of consciousness. Thus, concludes Zukav, "physics has become a branch of psychology, or perhaps the other way round. . . . physics is the study of the structure of consciousness."[5]

So both writers assert that the old, mechanistic model of nature must be replaced with an organic view in which all things, all events, all perceptions are interrelated, interconnected, and part of a unified whole. It is precisely this sense of the unity of the universe (and the interrelationship of all its parts) which Zukav and Capra put forward as the basis for their comparisons between the new physics and mysticism, and, more importantly, it is the lack of such an organic view which these writers see as the major shortcoming of biblical religions. Hence, if western culture will follow the lead of the latest science, the God of the Judeo-Christian tradition, the "ruler who directs the world from above" must be replaced by a "principle that controls everything from within."[6]

Notice that our theologians of the new physics do not talk very much about God. Despite all their references to mysticism they are saying in essence that science and religion converge upon a series of abstractions. For example, Capra argues that the new physics and the old mysticism are alike in that "all things are seen as interdependent and inseparable parts of this cosmic whole; as different manifestations of the same, ultimate reality."[7] Zukav summarizes similarly:

> We have come a long way from Galileo's experiments with falling bodies. Each step along the path has taken us to a higher level of abstraction: first to the creation of things that no one has ever seen (like electrons), and then to the abandonment of all attempts even to picture our abstractions.[8]

What Capra and Zukav offer at the interface of science and religion, East and West, is nothing more than an abstraction free of any color, character, or quality that one can envision: oneness, unity, the cosmic whole, the web of relationships, the principle that controls from within. Is it necessary, though, to replace the whole biblical tradition and its wealth of concrete symbols with such colorless abstractions? If science and religion can be brought into harmony only by sacrificing God, have we paid too high a price for the unification of consciousness?

Admittedly, if the God of the Judeo-Christian tradition were as shallow and one-dimensional as Capra and Zukav imply, then one might be willing to make such a sacrifice or at least to keep such a meddlesome God out of science so that the pursuit of truth could continue in a free and unfettered manner. Also, admittedly, a God built upon the Aristotelian model of the outside prime mover or even upon the political model of a ruler who directs the world from on high would be antithetical to science. These images of God, however, are not the only ones available within the Judeo-Christian tradition. In fact, Aristotle's prime mover is not biblical at all, and the conception of God as monarch cannot be lifted out of its specific context in the Bible.

The idea of a divine king or monarch did not arise easily or naturally within a culture which was originally nomadic. In fact, the God of the Bible arose out of opposition to the very notion of divine monarchy. That is a major theme of Exodus; the God of the Judeo-Christian faith emerged precisely in the midst of the struggle for freedom. The God of Abraham, Isaac, and Jacob, the God of Moses and the prophets, matured in the religion of the Late Bronze and Early Iron Ages among a people just settling into the small villages and towns in that region of the world now known as Israel and Jordan. When they finally reached the point in the evolution of their new nation that it seemed appropriate to appoint a king, they also appointed prophets to challenge and criticize the monarchs. It was this prophetic tradition which was honed and sharpened in the teachings and parables of Jesus. As he said to his closest disciples:

> You know that the rulers of the Gentiles lord it over them, and their great men exercise authority over them. It shall not be so among you; but whoever would be great among you must be your servant, and whoever would be first among you must be your slave.   (Matt. 20:25–27)

When God is depicted as a monarch, using such titles as Lord of Lords and King of Kings, such titles must be read in full awareness of the complementary servant imagery, so that the two sets of images, held in juxtaposition, convey a wholly new meaning.

When twentieth-century readers look back upon the Bible, they are looking back across six thousand years in which many a monarch has lifted biblical imagery out of context to legitimate the power and authority of monarchy and of many other forms of government, some much more worse than monarchy. At the same time, in this same history the egalitarian images have been used with equal effect by those who see God as the champion of freedom. From the Blacks of Africa who saw in the Exodus a sign of their own liberation from slavery to feminists of our own time who find in the Scriptures a signal of still deeper transformation in the relationships between the sexes, the Bible has been and continues to be a virtual source book for liberation movements of every kind.

Why is it that slaves and slave owners, monarchs and Marxists have found in the Scriptures such a rich source of symbols? The basic and fundamental reason for the continuing relevance of the Bible is precisely to be found in its view of God. When one looks at the whole of the Bible, one sees a God who is related to the world organically and dynamically. One does not find a single view of God fixed in any doctrine or frozen in any abstraction; one sees a living God who enters into direct and intimate relationship with the world.

This is stated just as emphatically in the Old Testament as it is in the New. In fact, the Bible opens with the most basic affirmation that God "created man in his own image; in the image of God he created him; male and female he created them." In other words, we are related to God in the most direct and intimate way. As God's own creatures we find the image and likeness of God in our own nature. This fundamental point is brought into even sharper focus in the New Testament where the figure of Jesus is put forward both as example and as archetype. If one looks for a symbol of the unity and interrelationship of all things, one need look no farther than the image of Christ suggested by the letter to the Colossians:

> He is the image of the invisible God, the first-born of all creation; for in him all things were created, in heaven and on earth, visible and invisible, whether thrones or dominions or principalities or authorities—all things were created through him and for him. He is before all things, and in him all things hold together.   (Col. 1:15–17)

I realize that readers who are put off by the theological imperialism of the Christian church may find in this passage a declaration of the supremacy of Jesus over all the other creatures. Anyone who has been confronted by the theological arrogance of the institutional church or the self-righteousness of individual Christians may be justified in drawing such a conclusion, but Paul's letter to the Colossians must be read alongside Paul's letter to the Philippians, in which Christ's claim to be a representative of all is specified as the very antithesis of arrogance and self-righteousness: "Though he was in the form of God, [Christ Jesus] did not count equality with God a thing to be grasped, but emptied himself, taking the form of a servant" (Phil. 2:6–7). In other words, there is nothing in the Bible which requires the view that God's rule is imposed upon creation from above. Even though many interpreters of the Bible, themselves occupying privileged positions in the various hierarchies of western society, have manipulated the text to justify their own standing and privilege, the central and unifying theme of Scripture is that all creatures are destined to share in God's justice and mercy. In creation, all things are equally characterized by God as good. Clearly, the web of their interrelationships extends beyond the human, beyond the animal, to encompass the whole material world.

In *The Dancing Wu Li Masters* Gary Zukav lifts up the image of the cosmic dance. He writes:

> A beautiful Hindu painting shows Lord Krishna dancing in the moonlight on the banks of the Yamuna. He moves in the center of a circle of fair Vraja women. They are all in love with Krishna

and they are dancing with him. Krishna is dancing with all the souls of the world—man is dancing with himself. To dance with god, the creator of all things, is to dance with ourselves. This is a recurrent theme of eastern literature. This is also the direction toward which the new physics, quantum mechanics and relativity, seems to point.[9]

Capra also picks up the image of the dance, using it to draw the lines between physics and mysticism.

> Modern physics, then, pictures matter not at all as passive and inert, but as being in a continuous dancing and vibrating motion. . . . In the words of a Taoist text:
>
>> The stillness in stillness is not the real stillness. Only when there is stillness in movement can the spiritual rhythm appear which pervades heaven and earth.[10]

There are a few references to the sacred dance in the Scriptures too, but the preferred imagery of the Bible lifts up the sacred song: "Sing to the Lord a new song" (Ps. 149:1). As envisioned by the psalm writer, the whole cosmos is caught up in a song of praise:

> Praise the LORD from the earth,
>   you sea monsters and all deeps,
> fire and hail, snow and frost,
>   stormy wind fulfilling his command!
>
> Mountains and all hills,
>   fruit trees and all cedars!
> Beasts and all cattle,
>   creeping things and flying birds!
>
> Kings of the earth and all peoples,
>   princes and all rulers of the earth!
> Young men and maidens together,
>   old men and children!
> Let them praise the name of the LORD.
>   (Ps. 148:7–13a)

When Gary Zukav looks at the world, he sees everything to be essentially in a state of dance, and he asserts that this is the same view that is arising out of physics: "According to particle physics, the world is fundamentally dancing energy."[11] In the image of the dance he finds a unifying metaphor which depicts the essential nature of all things, organic and inorganic, but why is the biblical metaphor any less appropriate? In the sacred song of praise envisioned by the psalm writer, the whole cosmos is caught up in the singing: "fire and hail, kings of the earth and all peoples." In this psalm the distinction between matter and antimatter, animate and inanimate, animal and human, is resolved in the all-encompassing song of praise.

Both Zukav and Capra assert that eastern mysticism and quantum mechanics are alike in offering a *dynamic* view of the world whereas the western view is that all things are *static*. They both assert that, in western religions, the universe is governed by God's absolute and unchanging laws, physical systems work like machines, and people are instructed to order their lives according to rigid and inflexible commandments handed down from the high God in heaven. By contrast, our theologians of the new physics argue, science and mysticism depict a universe caught up in a continual cycle of change and growth. Writes Zukav:

> Subatomic particles forever partake of this unceasing dance of annihilation and creation. In fact, subatomic particles *are* this unceasing dance of annihilation and creation. This twentieth-century discovery, with all its psychedelic implications, is not a new concept. In fact, it is very similar to the way that much of the earth's population, including the Hindus and the Buddhists, view their reality.
>
> Hindu mythology is virtually a large-scale projection into the psychological realm of microscopic scientific discoveries. Hindu deities such as Shiva and Vishnu continually dance the creation and destruction of universes while the Buddhist image of the wheel of life symbolizes the unending process of birth, death, and rebirth which is a part of the world of form, which is emptiness, which is form.[12]

Is this psychedelic? Is this mystical? Perhaps so, but the pattern of life, death, and rebirth is also the primary image of transformation in the Bible. Drawing upon the original images concerning birth, death, and renewal found especially in the prophets, this same pattern is amplified and expanded to become the one essential image of change in the New Testament. In fact, the story of Christ's life, death, and resurrection becomes the pattern for all creation. In his letter to the Romans Paul depicts the whole creation as being caught up in the birth pangs of a new age: "We know that the whole creation has been groaning in travail together until now; and not only the creation, but we ourselves" (Rom. 8:22–23). One cannot imagine a more powerful statement of the inner relationship of all things—the solidarity and at the same time the dynamism of a whole cosmos which Paul depicts as waiting "with eager longing" and which will be "set free from its bondage to decay and obtain the glorious liberty of the children of God" (Rom. 8:19, 21). Jesus himself cast the processes of life, death, and regeneration in the form of an extended analogy:

> Truly, truly, I say to you, unless a grain of wheat falls into the earth and dies, it remains alone; but if it dies, it bears much fruit. He who loves his life loses it, and he who hates his life in this world will keep it for eternal life.   (John 12:24–25)

Theologians have spent hundreds of years trying to unravel the paradox here presented by Jesus. Why Capra and Zukav, who are so attracted to the paradoxical elements in eastern religion, ignore the element of paradox in all the parables of Jesus eludes me. For example, Zukav and Capra both praise the Zen technique called the *koan* as an agent of change and transformation in Buddhist religion. Zukav writes:

> A *koan* is a puzzle which cannot be answered in ordinary ways because it is paradoxical. "What is the sound of one hand clapping?" is a Zen *koan*. Zen students are told to think unceasingly about a particular *koan* until they know the answer. There is no single correct answer to a *koan*. It depends upon the psychological state of the student.

> Paradoxes are common in Buddhist literature. Paradoxes are the places where our rational mind bumps into its own limitations. According to eastern philosophy in general, opposites, such as good-bad, beautiful-ugly, birth-death, and so on, are

"false distinctions." One cannot exist without the other. These are mental structures which we have created. These self-made and self-maintained illusions are the sole cause of paradoxes. To escape the bonds of conceptual limitation is to hear the sound of one hand clapping.[13]

Likewise the parables of Jesus cannot be reduced to a single dimension of meaning; they too are often nonsensical and paradoxical in relation to our commonsense view of the world. From the perspective of most people living in a culture of science and technology, the parables are paradoxical because they approach a level of understanding deeper than the popular thought forms of an industrialized society. As Zukav suggests is the case with the Buddhists, exactly so are the students of Christianity advised to contemplate the parables until their deeper meanings become apparent. Like a *koan*, a parable normally has no single correct interpretation, though, as we shall see, it is not accurate to say with Zukav that everything depends on the psychological state of the student. In the biblical view, reality cannot be reduced to a psychological state. Nevertheless, as Zukav asserts of the *koan*, so it is with the parables; these also stand above the ordinary categories and distinctions of static thought. The parables clearly transcend all conventional distinctions between good and bad, beautiful and ugly, birth and death. In fact, these socially and culturally mediated distinctions are what make the parables seem so paradoxical in the first place. To escape the normal limits of such time-bound distinctions is to see that whoever loves life loses it and that whoever hates life will keep it.

Since there are as many similarities between biblical religion and the new physics as there are between the new physics and the religions of the East, why is it that Capra and Zukav do not notice? Why is it that particle physics "forces" us toward eastern mysticism even as we are encouraged by these writers to abandon the God of Judaism and Christianity? If there is a difference between the texts cited by Zukav and Capra and similar texts from the Bible that affirm the unity and interrelationships of all things, it is quite simply this: their texts finally lead in a circle.

Following their lead we move outward, into science and into nature, so that in the end we can arrive back home with a deeper understanding of the self. In the gospel according to Zukav our destiny is simply to sing praises of the self. "Krishna is dancing with all the souls of the world—man is dancing with himself." By contrast, in the biblical view all things find their fulfillment in and through their relationship to the Creator.

Though they call it mysticism, Zukav and Capra have choreographed a dance to be performed at the funeral of God. They have offered nothing less than a religious argument for scientific atheism. Not content to let God die of natural causes, they hammer away at the God of the West, forcing the Deity into rhetorical corners from which there is clearly no escape. Systematically and relentlessly, they define the western God in such a way that one is forced to see East and West as polar opposites, so that, just as soon as one sees the similarities between physics and mysticism, in this same step one sees the God of the West as dead. By way of illustration, we have seen how essential it is that God be thoroughly identified with Greek dualism. Both Capra and Zukav peg their whole case against biblical religion on the assertion that it is rooted and grounded in dualism. Thus Zukav argues:

> The matter-energy dichotomy goes back at least as far as the Old Testament. Genesis portrays man as a sort of ceramic creation. God scoops up a handful of clay (matter) and breathes life (energy) into it. The Old Testament is a product of the western world (or the other way around). In the East, however, there never has been much philosophical or religious . . . confusion about matter and energy.[14]

Zukav's rendering of the creation story is a total misrepresentation. In the first place there are two verses in Genesis depicting the creation of humanity and reflecting the differing perspectives of at least two separate theological traditions. The first, already cited, gives no excuse whatever for the accusation that there is any confusion about energy and matter. "So God created man in his own image, in the image of God he created him" (Gen. 1:27). This verse emphasizes the close relationship be-

tween the divine and the human. There is no bifurcation between energy and matter, no separation of the material from the
spiritual. The whole human creature is shaped in God's own
image. The second verse is perhaps the one Zukav has in mind:
"The LORD God formed man of dust from the ground, and
breathed into his nostrils the breath of life; and man became a
living being" (Gen. 2:7). In the Hebrew language, however, "the
breath of life" is just as real, just as substantial as the dust of the
ground. Again, the image of God breathing into the nostrils of
the first homo sapiens emphasizes the intimacy of the human
and the divine. There is no thought of dualism here, no "confusion" about energy and matter. Just the opposite is true. The
book of Genesis and the whole Hebrew Bible constitute the
strongest possible argument for the unity of the material and
the spiritual. Zukav's reading of the Genesis story and the whole
biblical tradition is sadly misinformed.

In a similar vein he appeals to the New Testament to substan-
tiate his argument that the religion of the West is antithetical to
science. He reads the story of the risen Christ's appearances to
the Apostle Thomas as illustrative of this whole problem:

> Christ, following His resurrection, proved to Thomas (who be-
> came the proverbial "Doubting Thomas") that He really was
> He, risen from the dead, by showing Thomas His wounds. At
> the same time, however, Christ bestowed His special favor on
> those who believed Him *without proof.*

> Acceptance without proof is the fundamental characteristic of
> western religion. Rejection without proof is the fundamental
> characteristic of western science. In other words, religion has
> become a matter of the heart and science has become a matter
> of the mind. This regrettable state of affairs does not reflect the
> fact that, physiologically, one cannot exist without the other. . . .
> The Wu Li Masters know that "science" and "religion" are only
> dances, and that those who follow them are dancers. The danc-
> ers may claim to follow "truth" or claim to seek "reality," but the
> Wu Li Masters know better. They know that the true love of all
> dancers is dancing.[15]

Whatever the Wu Li Masters know, Zukav does not know the
meaning and purpose of Christ's appearance to Thomas. (This

narrative occurs in John 20:24–29.) It was written nearly seventy years after the crucifixion. At the time of its composition the Apostles, who had shared direct experience of the risen Christ, would not have been present to give an eyewitness account of the events being depicted. John's purpose in including this story (note that earlier Gospels do not mention the incident) is to convey the reality of the resurrection. At this time in history, Greek dualism *was* regarded as a serious problem for the church because some Christians were arguing that Jesus was a spiritual being, not a true human being with a real body. Therefore, in telling of this dramatic encounter between the risen Christ and one of the Apostles, John is making a case for the physical reality of the risen Christ, just as he had argued for the reality and humanity of Jesus. Modern readers may find the whole idea of bodily resurrection to be scientifically impossible, but that is a distinctly contemporary problem. John is not in any way making a case for blind belief. "Acceptance without proof is the fundamental characteristic of western religion," asserts Zukav. In fact, however, the effort to *prove* the existence of God has been taken up again and again by theologians of the western world. Throughout this long tradition the issue has not been joined on the one side by those who argue for "acceptance without proof" as opposed to those who insist that faith can be substantiated. The real issue is and always has been: what sort of substantiation is required; what foundation does one have for one's belief? "Have you believed because you have seen me?" asks Jesus. Here Jesus chides Thomas for ruling out the very possibility of belief without the actual experience of touching and feeling the risen body of Jesus. The problem being addressed in this passage is actually the one originally faced by *John's* contemporaries who had no hope of seeing Christ in the flesh. It is for this second-century audience that John quotes Jesus: "Blessed are those who have not seen and yet believe." Behind these words lies the realization that, if faith in Christ were contingent upon seeing and even touching his body, Christianity would have received its death warrant even before the Gospel of John was written.

The story about Thomas also has another purpose. It emphasizes the reality of Christ's presence. John's Gospel begins with the dramatic proclamation that in Christ "the word became flesh," and our passage is only one of many which amplify John's major theme. This notion, which theologians refer to as the incarnation, is the strongest possible argument against Greek dualism. In fact, it is the basis for a renewed sense of the direct, intrinsic relationship of scientific understanding and faith.

As John states in his famous prologue: "In the beginning was the Word, and the Word was with God, and the Word was God. He was in the beginning with God; all things were made through him, and without him was not anything made that was made." When we combine this insight with the notion of human life shaped in the image and likeness of God, we have the precise biblical grounds for asserting that the free and unfettered inquiry into the deepest mysteries of life may lead one toward direct knowledge of God, and we have the exact rebuttal required of Capra's proposal that the "ruler who directs the world from above" must be replaced by "a principle that controls everything from within."[16]

As our brief review of biblical theology indicates, God cannot and should not be caricatured as a ruler who controls things from a remote position in heaven; God is clearly envisioned as present in all the processes of life. As Tillich insisted to Einstein, it is not at all clear that conceiving of God as an abstraction—a *principle* that controls everything from within—represents an improvement over the concrete, personal images of the Scriptures. In my own view it accords much better with nature and with the deepest insights of science to imagine God as a person with whom one has a relationship rather than as a principle that "controls everything from within." In fact, to be held in the constant control of an abstract principle seems closer to the static and mechanistic view that these writers so violently reject. Speaking metaphorically, it is far preferable to embrace and to be embraced by an all-loving God than to be caught up in an impersonal process of nature.

The Bible does not assert that we have direct or total knowledge of God. As Paul puts it, we see God as through a clouded mirror. Yet in moments of insight and in occasions of grace there is hope of one day seeing God "face to face." In the gospel according to the Tao, what we finally see is our own image in the mirror and nothing more than our own image.

Standing squarely within the tradition of scientific atheism, Zukav and Capra believe that their understanding of both science and theology constitutes a higher view of humanity. Since the distinctions between subjective and objective, mind and matter, mental and physical realities have dissolved, we can no longer conceive of ourselves as "passive witnesses" to the unfolding wonders of nature. We now conceive ourselves to be part of the cosmos and the cosmos to be a creation of the self. Thus Zukav concludes, "The Cogs in the Machine have become the Creators of the Universe."[17] However, the mechanistic notion of humanity as a mere cog in the cosmic machine has never been a conclusion one could draw from the religious literature of the West. To be sure, some early *scientific* theories may have implied such a limited and narrow view, but the biblical witness is clearly at variance with any such conception. The Old Testament pictures God's people as creatures who have been shaped in God's own image, destined to be drawn into a still closer and more intimate "covenant" with the Creator. In the New Testament the community of faith is seen as the very body of Christ. We are the very joints and ligaments of Christ's body in the world. Also, since Christ is, with God, the co-creator, we have a direct, personal role in the ongoing process of creation. In Judaism and perhaps more concretely in Christianity, humanity is clearly seen as a partner with God in creation so that, by any standard of measurement or comparison, the biblical tradition offers an equally "high" view of humanity and its role in the cosmos. The Bible provides just as much verification for the immanence of God as anything Zukav or Capra have discovered at the interface of the new physics and eastern mysticism. Moreover the Bible retains an emphasis upon God's transcendence. The Judeo-Christian tradition insists that God is not simply a figment of the human imagination or a product of the human mind, and this is, of course, the source of its prophetic power as well as its ethical subtlety.

While Capra and Zukav see in particle physics the same patterns of creation and destruction originally stated in the biblical themes of life, death, and resurrection, their formulation provides no basis for what is known in western thought as destiny or purpose. Like the spontaneous birth and death of a proton, life seems to come from nowhere and return to nowhere. In mysticism we have no forward motion, no sense of progress, no ultimate destination. We may be part of a cosmic whole, but in this web of chance, since every part is related equally and without distinction to every other part, the identity of all things dissolves into an illusion. If one is all and all is one, each individual signifies nothing. Zukav takes this woeful aspect of the mystic vision and puts it forward as mysticism's greatest virtue:

> A vital aspect of the enlightened state is the experience of an all-pervading unity. "This" and "that" no longer are separate entities. They are different *forms* of the same thing. Everything is a *manifestation*. It is not possible to answer the question, "Manifestation of *what?*" because the "what" is that which is beyond words, beyond concept, beyond form, beyond even space and time. Everything is a manifestation of that which is. That which is, is. Beyond these words lies the experience; the experience is that which is.

> The forms through which that which is manifests itself are each and every one of them perfect. *We* are manifestations of that which is. *Everything* is a manifestation of that which is. Everything and everybody is exactly and perfectly what it is.

A fourteenth-century Tibetan Buddhist, Longchenpa, wrote:

> Since everything is but an apparition
> Perfect in being what it is,
> Having nothing to do with good or bad,
> Acceptance or rejection,
> One may well burst out in laughter.

We may say, "God's in His heaven and all's well with the world," except that according to the enlightened view, the world couldn't be any other way. It is neither well nor not well. It

simply is what it is. What it is is perfectly what it is. It couldn't
be anything else. It is perfect. I am exactly and perfectly who I
am. You are perfect. You are exactly and perfectly who
you are.[18]

Christian theology also speaks of the ultimate as being beyond words, beyond concept, beyond form, beyond even space
and time. Within the major religions of the West, that which is
has a name, YHWH, the unpronounceable name, the paradoxical riddle given to Moses at the burning bush—"I am who I
am." This same God, the God of Abraham, Isaac, and Jacob, the
God of Jesus, has a purpose for creation: that all things may
share in God's own creativity, sovereignty, and love; that all may
participate with God in the beauty of creation; and that in this
relationship with the Creator all may have their own being affirmed, not denied.

A large part of Capra's and Zukav's misunderstanding of
western religion is rooted in their misreading of words like "purpose," "plan," and "destiny." They seem frozen into the view that
God's purpose is to issue arbitrary commands and unbending
laws. Both writers speak as though God enjoys issuing orders
from on high; and this is what they find most objectionable in
the monarchical images of God.

Moving from the observation that some modern physicists
have rejected the very notion of fundamental law in nature,
Capra muses:

> The notion of fundamental laws of nature was derived from the
> belief in a divine lawgiver which was deeply rooted in the
> Judaeo-Christian tradition. In the words of Thomas Aquinas:
>
>> There is a certain Eternal Law, to wit, Reason, existing in
>> the mind of God and governing the whole universe.
>
> This notion of an eternal, divine law of nature greatly influ-
> enced Western philosophy and science. Descartes wrote about
> the "laws which God has put into nature," and Newton believed
> that the highest aim of his scientific work was to give evidence
> of the "laws impressed upon nature by God." In modern phys-
> ics, a very different attitude has now developed. Physicists have
> come to see that all their theories of natural phenomena, includ-

ing the "laws" they describe, are creations of the human mind; properties of our conceptual map of reality, rather than of reality itself.[19]

There are two great flaws in this argument. First, there is a problem with the science. It is true enough that the so-called laws of nature are creations of the human mind, but that leaves open the question as to whether there is any correspondence between the theoretical constructions we use to organize our impressions of the world and the world itself. There is no consensus in the scientific community that the laws we draft are *merely* mental constructs. That, after all, was what Einstein devoted so much of his energy debating with his colleagues. He was speaking to the point when he asserted, "God does not play dice with the world." Yet even the dice follow certain laws and patterns of probability as they fall. Chance is what happens as the laws intersect; Einstein knew that if he had enough information about the exact force and direction in which the dice were thrown he could predict the results in advance every time, and that has *something* to do with the way things really are. To be sure Einstein would not have been so certain about the dice if he had not succeeded so brilliantly in exposing the orderly patterns that are contained within his famous formula, $E = MC^2$. Admittedly, one cannot offer a rationally coercive proof that the order we discern is the order that exists. By itself, science cannot decide this question; this is precisely the point at which we cross over from science to religion.

This brings us to the second flaw in Capra's argument: there is also a grave error in his theology. True enough, both Newton and Descartes saw God as a lawgiver, and they both succeeded masterfully at integrating the best science of their age with the best theology. Yet both science and theology have changed in the last two hundred years. Thomas Aquinas does not hold a monopoly in the world of Christian thought. Now theologians talk about process as much as they talk about law; they emphasize the elements of dynamism as much as the elements of order; and, above all, they affirm the grace and mercy of God beyond the juridical role of divine lawmaker. Moreover, as we reflect back upon the biblical roots of western theism, we know that God is not *fundamentally* a lawgiver at all. On the contrary, God is a Creator who calls all creatures to a life of creativity. God did not create humanity in order to have an opportunity of imposing all sorts of rules and regulations from above. The only reason law came into play at all was that human "creativity" had a way of getting out of hand; human freedom often led this species in destructive paths. "You shall not kill" and all the other commandments are not fundamental to creation; they were given by God only by way of reminding this species that, as creatures of God, it is our nature to create, not to destroy. Need I add that Jesus saw his own mission as a direct answer to all forms of legalism, formalism, and authoritarianism in religion? For Jesus, God is known by faith as the giver of grace. The law is both fulfilled and surpassed in the love which holds all things together, things in heaven and things on earth.

In the course of his argument about the law, Capra refers to Joseph Needham's study of Chinese science and civilization. He quotes Needham approvingly:

> In the Chinese worldview the harmonious cooperation of all beings arose, not from the orders of a superior authority external to themselves, but from the fact that they were all parts in a hierarchy of wholes forming a cosmic pattern, and what they obeyed were the internal dictates of their own natures."[20]

Yet the whole purpose of the law in biblical religion is precisely to clarify the fundamental point that it is *in our nature* to enter into closer relationship with a God who has created and is continually recreating the entire cosmos. To the extent that Zukav and Capra have succeeded in showing the relationship between physics and eastern mysticism, their books also show, albeit inadvertently, the deep parallels between the religions of the East and those of the West. Though they do not intend to make the point, their books provide substantial support for the view that a true reunion between science and religion will also involve some very provocative conversations across the fences separating the world's great religions.

Like all the apostles of scientific atheism, Capra and Zukav actually succeed in making a case not for the final rejection of the religion of the West but for a renewed appreciation of its neglected truth. The God of the West is not dead; on the contrary, this same God is alive and well, awaiting rediscovery by those who dare pursue the truth freed of every false distinction separating the realm of science from the realm of faith.

8.
CONCLUSION
Toward a New Theism

Though theology today is characterized by diversity, perhaps even disarray, there is one conclusion in which the vast majority of theologians agree. The classic proofs for the existence of God have failed. Not only that, the solid majority of world-class theologians maintain that further attempts to prove God's existence are futile. Not only do the traditional proofs fail to answer the objections posed by philosophers and scientists writing from a position outside the theological circle, but also the proofs are defeated by objections put forward from within. As Paul Tillich summarizes, "There can be little doubt that the arguments [for the existence of God] are a failure. . . . It would be a great victory for Christian apologetics if the words 'God' and 'existence' were very definitely separated."[1] Though few would go so far as Tillich does in his provocative attempt to turn the failure of the traditional proofs into a positive principle of theology itself, still nearly all would agree with Karl Barth that the very attempt to move on the wings of logic alone to any real knowledge of God is theologically suicidal. Most theologians today would echo the conclusion drawn long ago by Søren Kierkegaard who wrote satirically

> With what industrious zeal, with what sacrifice of time, of diligence, of writing materials, the speculative philosophers in our time have labored to get a strong and complete proof of the existence of God! But in the same degree that the excellence of the proof increases, certitude seems to decrease.[2]

To be sure, Roman Catholic theologians still work under the authority of the First Vatican Council, which affirmed as dogma "that the one and true God our creator and Lord can be known through the creation by the natural light of human reason."[3] Yet in the years since Vatican I the philosophical supports for that dogma have disintegrated, and some Catholic theologians are openly defiant. Writes Hans Küng in his most lucid book, *Does God Exist?*, "It must be admitted that, in so far as they seek to prove something, the proofs of God are meaningless."[4] At the same time, Küng and many others try to salvage the traditional arguments. If they are meaningless as proofs, still Küng concludes:

> In so far as they bring God into the discussion, they are very meaningful. As definite answers they are inadequate, but as open questions they are irrecusable. There is no doubt that the *probative character of the proofs of God is finished* today, *but their content remains important.*[5]

At first reading such efforts to rescue the failed arguments may sound like theological double-talk. Can one seriously suppose that one learns anything from a series of failed proofs except the futility of any further effort in the same direction? If the leaky bucket will not hold water, why try to rescue it for any further disappointing trips to the well? In what follows I will examine several such rescue efforts, not so much in order that we might repair the old proofs but to see whether we can find in the wreckage of the old any helpful suggestions which may serve as a point of departure in the construction of a new proof altogether.

As we have seen, Tillich turns the traditional arguments upon themselves, and he believes that every attempt to prove God's existence represents an effort to move from the world, which is known, to God, who is unknown.

> Every argument derives conclusions from something that is given about something that is sought. In arguments for the existence of God the world is given and God is sought. . . . But, if we derive God from the world, he cannot be that which transcends the world infinitely.[6]

Hence, concludes Tillich, every argument for God is founded upon a contradiction. To construct a view of God out of materials contained within the world cannot add anything of substance to what we already know of the world. Thus the arguments for God do not provide answers to the riddle of existence, but they do express the *"question* of God" which is implied by our own existence. In other words, Tillich rescues the old arguments by turning them around one hundred and eighty degrees; he sees them no longer as *answers* to the questions of life but as themselves reflecting the very deepest and most provocative of *questions*. "The arguments for the existence of God analyze the human situation in such a way that the question of God appears possible and necessary."[7]

In Anselm's classic statement of the so-called "ontological argument," the existence of God was derived from the very *idea* of a supreme being. The ontological proof tries to move from the very notion of a being "greater than which none other can be conceived" to the actual existence of such a being. The hinge of the argument, so stated, is that a supreme being which exists in the mind alone would be excelled by an identical being which takes up an actual place in reality. Immanuel Kant is generally thought to have unhinged this argument by showing that existence is not a property that can be attributed to an abstract idea. In fact, Kant further argued that it was impossible for science, as well as for theology, to move from the realm of thought to the realm of objective reality. The mere fact that we think something exists does not prove that it is so. Kant saw that our knowledge of the material world is limited to those sensory impressions that are organized and presented to our consciousness by the lens of thought. We have no direct access to an objective reality which may be shown to exist "out there." (Clearly this conclusion of Kant anticipates the very similar conclusions of twentieth-century physics. Our knowledge of the material world has been shown to be as limited and incomplete as our knowledge of God.)

However, if the ontological argument cannot be used to establish the existence of a supreme being, it does represent, for Tillich, the acknowledgment of what he called the "unconditional"; to put it another way, our very human sense of finitude impresses upon us the possibility of the infinite; our awareness that we exist in time suggests the possibility of the eternal. Tillich asserts that while the ontological argument fails as a proof it functions symbolically, suggesting that there is "an unconditional element" to be found within the conditions of existence. Tillich continues:

> Modern secularism is rooted largely in the fact that the unconditional element in the structure of reason and reality no longer was seen and that therefore the idea of God was imposed on the mind as a "strange body." This produced first heteronomous subjection and then autonomous rejection. The destruction of the ontological *argument* is not dangerous. What is dangerous is the destruction of an approach which elaborates the possibility of the question of God.[8]

Tillich affirms a similar validity for the cosmological and teleological arguments. These too represent an attempt to move from one level or dimension of reality to another. In this case certain known features of the world are put forward as proof of a first cause or final source of meaning. Again reason tries to follow a path that leads from the creation toward the Creator, and again these arguments fail. Still, Tillich argues, they have a role to play in our analysis of the human situation. It is not the force of logic but anxiety about the end and meaning of life which is reflected in these arguments. It is anxiety which "drives man toward the question of our infinite, unthreatened ground of meaning."[9]

Faced by the stark fact of our own finitude, we are driven to ask whether there is any meaning in life beyond the limits of our own mortality. Hence, while nothing in the world serves as sure and certain evidence of a supreme being, the world does raise the supreme question of the ground of being. We think Cancer! or Nuclear War! and begin asking whether life rests on any sure foundation. Tillich sees the possibility of a divine ground, goal, and support for life as arising from the threats which we all experience in life itself. In sum, Tillich does not say that God is logically *proven;* rather, the possibility of God is *suggested* by the very conditions of our existence.

Catholic theologian Hans Küng moves in a similar direction, rejecting the claims to certitude put forward in the ontological, teleological, and cosmological arguments for God but insisting that these traditional arguments do offer "food for thought." Though the ontological proof fails to move from the realm of thought to the existence of a "most perfect or absolutely necessary being," still it can be taken seriously "less as a proof than as an expression of trusting faith." Küng finds the ontological argument of value in focusing our attention upon God as "a supreme fullness of being."[10]

Likewise, the teleological argument, which moves from the meanings we find in the world toward God as the source of meaning, fails as a proof but does tend to support one's sense that life is meaningful. Küng asks, "If God is understood as ultimately bestowing meaning . . . would not the acceptance of an end of all ends *ipso facto* mean . . . the acceptance of God? This would be an acceptance . . . of God's existence without a proof of God."[11] Finally, Küng finds in the cosmological proof no coercive argument for a first cause. For, as we have seen, the law of cause and effect has itself been subjected to the most withering criticisms. One cannot argue back along a faulty chain of cause and effect toward sure knowledge of a first cause. Nevertheless, while it may not be logically necessary, it may be

> reasonable to assume a first cause of all. . . . If God is understood as ultimately founding and causing, would not the acceptance of a cause of all causes *ipso facto* mean . . . the acceptance of God? This would be an acceptance . . . of God's existence without a proof of God.[12]

Küng then proceeds to define "acceptance of God" as equivalent to entering into a relationship of fundamental trust. That is to say, belief is not and never should have been defined as an act of the mind alone; it is just as much an act of the will and a movement of the emotions. In this context Küng recalls that, while Kant undercut the foundations of the traditional arguments for God, he put forward a new argument of his own which was secured in practical rather than theoretical reason. In fact, the notion of God comes most powerfully into play at the borderline of ethics and theology, at the boundary of action and thought. Küng writes:

> The idea of God is indeed a necessary theoretical borderline concept, which, like a distant star, cannot be reached in the process of knowing, but nevertheless can be aimed at as an ideal goal. As we need the concept of the soul (self) and of the world (as embodiment of all appearances), in order to regulate and systematize our psychological and cosmological knowledge, we need in principle also the idea of God, in order to combine harmoniously internal and external events in a comprehensive unity.[13]

Here Küng draws upon Kant in defining God as "a concept which completes and crowns the whole of human knowledge. Its objective reality cannot be proved, but also cannot be disproved, by merely speculative reason."[14]

Yet, while the existence of God cannot be established by any act of reason, belief in God can, according to Küng, be verified and justified as a reasonable decision. To believe in God is to commit oneself in an attitude of fundamental trust to the world as meaningful and to continue searching for the meaning to its very source. Such a faithful commitment is, of course, the very first step for both scientists and theologians. To believe in God is to trust that the universe is open to discovery, that God is revealed in the depths of creation.

> Yet unfortunately the "depth" (or "height") of a truth and the certainty with which it is accepted by man are in inverse ratio. The more banal the truth ("truism," "platitude") the greater the certainty. The more significant the truth (for instance aesthetic, moral and religious truth by comparison with arithmetical) the slighter the certainty. For the "deeper" the truth is for me, the more must I lay myself open to it, inwardly prepare myself, attune myself to it intellectually, voluntarily, emotionally, in order to reach that genuine "certainty" which is somewhat different from assured "security." A *deep* truth, for me outwardly uncertain, menaced by doubts, which presupposes a generous commitment on my part, can possess much more cognitive value than a certain—or even an "absolutely certain"—*banal* truth $(2 + 2 = 4)$.[15]

For Küng it is clear, trust in God and an attitude of fundamental trust toward reality itself are closely related, if not identical.

In this respect his theology may be compared to that of Til-

lich who defined faith as a state of ultimate concern. For both
these theologians, belief may be more nearly compared to a loving commitment to another person than to an act of intellectual
speculation. That is to say, belief is a state which involves the
whole person in an encounter with what is most real and ultimate. Faith weaves its patterns in and through the cloth of
thought; it colors sensory experience and inspires action, including the act of science. Yet faith transcends these various dimensions of human consciousness, holding them all together.

From this perspective it becomes apparent that the traditional proofs have failed, not because they attempted to prove
so much but because they tried to accomplish too little. The
classical arguments for God of necessity were built upon the
foundations of Greek dualism (later reinforced by the scientific
dualism of Descartes and Newton). Accordingly, in order to
prove God one had to cross the barrier which dualistic thought
had erected between the ideal and the real, between body and
soul, between reason and emotion, between objective and subjective. With reality itself so bifurcated and so divided, it is little
wonder that no logical argument or turn of phrase could breach
the gaps that had opened up at the very heart and center of
human consciousness. What the science of the twentieth century
has done more than anything else is to dismantle the whole system of dualistic thought, first in science and later, by inference,
in philosophy and theology, so that it becomes increasingly apparent that the classical proofs for God are to be regarded not
so much as unworkable as they are unnecessary. As we continue
our review of the work being done by theologians of the late
twentieth century, we can see how this new situation suggests a
whole new set of criteria for anyone interested in finding substantiation for faith.

John Macquarrie comes closer to a full realization of the present situation than any of the theologians we have discussed thus
far. Yet he also tries to turn the failed proofs to a more comprehensive purpose. While agreeing that the traditional arguments
do not succeed in providing logically coercive proof for God,
Macquarrie writes:

Nevertheless, there remains some value in (these) arguments. The ontological argument shows that an idea of God or perfect being is somehow native to the human mind, so that man has, in Schleiermacher's expression, a "sense and taste for the infinite." The cosmological argument articulates an awareness of the mystery of existence and proceeds from what E. L Mascall has called "the capacity for contemplative wondering." The teleological argument draws our attention to the amazingly complex structure of the universe and its potentialities for bringing forth living and even personal beings; and Hume's point about the immanence of the potentialities in nature, made at a time when God was conceived in starkly, transcendent terms, seems less important in a time when we have to some extent recovered a sense of God's closeness to the world. Thus, even if the proofs fail as proofs, they may retain enough residual value to form a cumulative argument for the reasonableness of belief in God.[16]

Macquarrie then draws our attention to the fact that proponents of the various arguments for God did not arrive at their faith through a process of logic or reason. There was a prior faith rooted in personal experience, training, or tradition. The rational proof merely elucidated to the mind what was first believed. Macquarrie rightly sees the task of theology as one of pressing through the logic of a given proof to its experiential foundations. Hence he argues that the function of theology should be *descriptive* rather than *deductive*.

This descriptive type of . . . theology does not *prove* anything, but it *lets us see*, for it brings out into the light the basic situation in which faith is rooted, so that we can then see what its claims are. Incidentally, it may well be that this kind of procedure will be far more effective as an apologetic than the old attempts to demonstrate by rational argument, but if we proceed by way of description rather than demonstration, we are asking the person addressed to *look with us* at the phenomena. There is a measure of participation here which is more likely than an abstract argument to lead into a genuine understanding of a religious faith, for this latter is never in any case a merely theoretical belief.[17]

Note that Macquarrie moves beyond the modest attempts to retrieve some useful shards of truth from the failed proofs. He uses the failure of the old arguments as the starting point for a wholly new approach to God.

He puts forward three simple tests of validity for any theological affirmation. First, faith statements must be internally consistent. One cannot simply spin off a random series of affirmations from one's individual imagination. The theologian must put forward a "unifying vision of man's life in its widest setting." That leads directly to Macquarrie's next criteria which is in fact a corollary of the first. Second, theological affirmations must pass the test of "coherence with our other well founded beliefs, derived from the sciences, from history, and other disciplines." Macquarrie rejects the notion that religious faith can be constructed in a vacuum. He recognizes, with Marx and Freud very much in the background of his thought, that all religious belief arises out of its psychological and social setting. Religious teachings must be studied in their particular context and tested against the standards of veracity used in related disciplines. This brings us to Macquarrie's third criteria: because religious truth emerges in dialectical relation to all the other elements in a changing culture, one should look for flexibility and openness to change in any faith system. "Finality and fixity are signs of error. There must be room for development, for the process of advancing into truth."[18]

Inherent consistency, coherence with knowledge arising out of related disciplines, and openness to change and growth—these criteria provide for both the reconstruction of theology in the light of modern science and the standard of verification against which all faith claims can be tested. Clearly Macquarrie's agenda for a descriptive theology does suggest that a more persuasive case for theism can be constructed. For, if the old arguments were conceived primarily as operations of the intellect, we now know how narrow a range of reality the intellect can encompass. Note that Macquarrie does not abandon reason as a source of truth; he simply asserts that reason cannot be held up as the final criterion of truth. Instead he sees truth mediated through the emotions as well as the mind, through personal and social relationships as well as the intellect, through structures of society as well as structures of thought. Like Tillich, Macquarrie never claims that his criteria for the verification of faith will lead to a new proof for God, but it should now be evident that an approach to God constructed along these lines allows for an argument grounded more broadly in the whole of human life, not simply in the life of the mind. By the same token, the new argument is grounded more deeply in the whole field of human knowledge, in the work of science as well as in the work of the spirit.

Moving in similar directions and in still closer symmetry with science is the work of Thomas F. Torrance. This Scottish theologian draws freely from the work of Albert Einstein and the scientist/philosopher Michael Polanyi to uncover the deep similarities between natural science and theology. In moving from the mechanistic and dualistic views of the seventeenth century, he argues, both these related disciplines were caught up in the same process of transformation. Whereas science and theology have been seen as completely separate endeavors, there now appears to be a deep coherence between the two realms of thought. So Torrance titles a recent book, *Transformation and Convergence in the Frame of Knowledge* (1984). The very suggestion that there may be a single frame of knowledge encompassing both the natural sciences and theology is startling and, if true, revolutionary in its implications.

Torrance shows convergence in the frame of theological and scientific knowledge both in his description of the process of discovery and in his understanding of how the two disciplines share a common faith. In drawing these connections Torrance builds upon the work of his two scientific authorities, Einstein and Polanyi. As these scientists depict their own work, scientific research resembles what theologians refer to as revelation. That is to say, the real breakthroughs do not come as a result of reason or logic. Instead, the scientist attends to nature and observes its passing phenomena with a basic trust that nature will disclose its deepest secrets. It is through a process of inquiry which Einstein described as "purely intuitive, not itself of a logical nature" that the greatest theories emerge, including Einstein's own theories of relativity. Hence, according to Einstein, "there is 'no logical path' to the laws of nature – 'only intuition resting on sympathetic understanding of experience, can reach them.'"[19]

Science and theology share a common faith that creation is

responsive to our hunger for understanding. We first believe that nature is intelligible and then set out faithfully to discover its deepest secrets. Yet there is no logical reason to believe that the universe is comprehensible. No one can prove that medical research will eventually lead to a cure for cancer, but one proceeds in faith. Moving forward in faith, one often finds that faith is supported by the disclosure of things unknown and new.

Torrance sees in Einstein's account of the process of discovery an exact analogue to the Christian doctrine of justification by faith. In science, as in the life of the spirit, the greatest rewards are those received as a gift. Nature's truths are not accessible at the command of the will or at the call of the intellect; they are disclosed to the researcher who proceeds by faith, remaining open to discovery at the outer edge of knowledge. As Einstein said of the discoveries of his fellow physicist Max Planck, "The emotional state which enables such achievements is similar to that of the religious person or the person in love."[20]

Torrance extrapolates three of Einstein's most characteristic logia by way of illustrating the "massive new synthesis" which he sees emerging at the interface of natural science and theology. "God does not play dice" was, according to Torrance, Einstein's way of affirming the objective intelligibility of the universe. Einstein's very success in formulating his great theories of relativity, not so much through any logical process of inductive or deductive reason but in a great leap of the imagination, has demonstrated more powerfully than any other event in the science of this century that we have seen the end of all debilitating dualism. With Einstein it becomes apparent that reality is no longer bifurcated into separate realms of time and space, energy and matter. Everything takes its place in one continuum. Likewise, in Einstein, Torrance also sees the end of all mechanistic conceptions of nature in which the human observer is seen as separate and distinct from an inhuman universe. Increasingly the universe appears to be accessible to understanding, and it now seems possible to achieve what has been regarded as an impossibility since the time of Kant; namely, a breakthrough in the once impenetrable barriers separating the subjective and the objective. Thus Torrance sees in Einstein's denial of the dice-playing God an affirmation about creation which can be traced back directly to its biblical root:

> It hardly needs to be pointed out that such a view is much more congenial to classical Christian understanding of the relation of God to the world he has made than the positivist outlook which rests upon the bifurcation of nature into mind and body, subject and object, and the mechanistic conception of the universe to which that gave rise. It is in fact Christian teaching about creation and incarnation which produced the concept of contingent intelligibility upon which all modern science now rests, while it is the transcendence and oneness of God, the creative Source of all rational order, which gave unity, identity, objectivity and comprehensiveness to the space-time medium in which we and all created reality are bracketed together in one world.[21]

Torrance then moves forward to capture the theological implications of Einstein's familiar aphorism: "God does not wear his heart on his sleeve." Even as Einstein affirmed the intelligibility of the universe, he still maintained in his maturity what he suspected even as a child, that the deepest laws and secrets of nature were not of the surface. When Einstein looked at the compass at the age of five and found its movements miraculous, he drew the conclusion which remained with him throughout his adult life. "Something deeply hidden had to be behind things."[22] For Einstein this did not mean abandoning the scientific method or sacrificing reason in order to explain natural phenomena by any supernatural or occult causes. Rather it meant that in approaching the natural world

> we have to think in a dimension of ontological depth in which the surface of things is coordinated with a deep, invisible, intelligible structure. . . . Really to know is to be in touch with a depth of reality which has the capacity for disclosure beyond what we can anticipate or imagine.[23]

Torrance finds in Einstein's aphorism a scientific equivalent to the Christian understanding of Christ's own nature as the Son of God. In Christ, the divine and the human are not seen as separate and distinct elements related back respectively to the supernatural and the natural. Rather, the elements of Christ's humanity and divinity are thought of "conjunctively" as part of one indivisible whole. "God does not wear his heart on his sleeve" reflects one scientist's discovery of the same multidimensional unity which Christian theology has tried to convey in its teachings about Jesus as the Christ.

Finally, Torrance reflects theologically upon Einstein's often repeated affirmation, "God is deep but not devious." Even while it is true that the laws of nature reveal themselves to the human imagination only in a dimension of depth, Einstein's rejection of any "devious" element in nature comes very close to an explicit scientific encounter with the just and loving God of the Judeo-Christian faith. As Torrance writes:

> The immanent order hidden behind the intricate and often baffling interconnections which we find in the universe is essentially trustworthy, for in spite of all that might appear to the contrary when we come up against sets of events for which there seems to be no rational explanation, the universe is not arbitrary or evil. God does not play tricks with us.[24]

As I suggested in the opening chapter of this book, it is more than coincidental that light plays such a critical role both in the science of relativity and in the symbolism of theology. Just as light appears in Einstein's famous formula ($E = MC^2$) as the very image of nature's dynamism and constancy, so light appears in Christian theology as a ranking symbol of God's dynamic yet constant presence in the world. Of course Einstein realized that the fundamental faith of science cannot be derived either from research or reason alone. As Torrance puts it, "While in the logical sense such an order in the universe is neither verifiable nor falsifiable, it remains the most persistent of all our scientific convictions for without it there could be no science at all."[25] If, then, both scientists and theologians proceed by faith, where does that lead us in our search for a new *proof* for the existence of God?

In the preface to the second edition of the *Critique of Pure Reason* Kant wrote, "I have therefore found it necessary to deny *knowledge,* in order to make room for *faith.*" That statement and the dualism which it implies go a long way toward explaining both the rise and the fall of traditional arguments for belief in God. For, if there is a common element in the ontological, cosmological, and teleological arguments, it is precisely their common attempt to cross the barriers that were once believed to separate the several dimensions of human consciousness. If it were to be demonstrated that God is, in fact, the organizing principle of reality (in biblical terms the Beginning and the End, the Alpha and the Omega), then it must be shown that the same supreme being which the mind conceives actually exists as an objective reality, holding a supreme position in the world of sight and sound. Crossing the barriers between the ideal and the real was precisely what the ontological arguments tried to accomplish.

Similarly, if we find certain patterns and designs in the world of sensory experience, be they as diverse as the movement of the moon or the flight of a moon rocket, then it must be shown that these same patterns can be traced back to a patternmaker. In the face of the often chaotic and random realities we encounter in the world of sight and sound, can we draw the logical connections that will make clear how all things do in fact fall into place under the rule of a just and loving God? Crossing the barrier between the realm of sensation and the realm of the spirit was precisely what the cosmological and teleological arguments tried to accomplish. Yet the same dualism that made this whole enterprise necessary also made it impossible. For, once you have put brackets around the operations of pure reason and have separated the life of the mind from bodily sensation, in that same step any God which can be conceived by the mind is bracketed off from the world of sight and sound, touch, taste, and smell.

The same difficulty presents itself in the rise and fall of arguments from design. As we have seen in our discussion of Darwin, the whole notion of design in nature was actually an attempt to cross the gap between the natural and the supernatural. If nature is defined as a great impersonal machine and

God is conceived as a Supreme Being or Person, then there must be some mediating concept that will make clear how an impersonal process in nature can still be conceived as the act of a personal God. The argument from design was a noble attempt to cross the barrier between the natural and supernatural, the personal and the impersonal, the spiritual and the material.

As dualistic thinking became an unquestioned assumption of science and theology and as it penetrated even more deeply into the structures of consciousness, it eventually became apparent that reason could not rescue God from banishment to the realm of disembodied spirituality. Also, as science was able to explain more and more of the great mysteries of life, there was perceived to be less and less room for God. The conclusion that had been drawn early on by the skeptic and scientist Pierre-Simon de Laplace became a rule of thumb for all scientific endeavor. When asked by Napoleon why there was no mention of God in his *Celestial Mechanics,* Laplace replied, "Sire, I had no need of the hypothesis." Finally, these tendencies in science reached so far as to encompass theology itself, culminating in Bonhoeffer's complete surrender to scientific atheism, "It is becoming evident that everything gets along without 'God'—and, in fact, just as well as before."[26] Karl Barth pronounced the whole enterprise of natural theology to be founded upon a fundamental flaw. In Barth's theology it was simply impossible to move across the barriers from the natural to the supernatural. From the human point of view knowledge of God is quite simply impossible. It is supremely ironic that, as the theologians surrendered more and more territory to a godless science, the same dualism which lay at the source of the conflict between religion and science gradually began to collapse of its own weight, or, rather, it became more and more apparent that dualism is quite simply *unscientific.*

In fact the history of science since Darwin can be written around this single theme, as dualism withers away in one discipline after another. Since Darwin, the whole evolution of life has been interpreted not as the result of a plan imposed from above but as a miracle arising from within nature itself. Since Marx, the structures of society have been seen increasingly not as a pattern imposed upon history by a God who rules from on high but as a dialectical process that encompasses all nations and all peoples. As Marx revealed the interrelationships between various classes and various periods of history, Freud revealed the interconnecting structures of human consciousness itself. Since Freud, the human being is seen not as a soul temporarily encamped in a body but as an organic whole in which various dimensions of consciousness are inseparably related. Finally, since Einstein, in physics the very strongest distinctions of dualistic thought have been defeated. Relativity theory and quantum mechanics have revealed the fundamental distinctions between energy and matter, time and space to be illusory. Thus the real irony is that, at the very moment the theologians have abandoned hope of ever bridging the gaps in human consciousness or crossing the barriers in human thought, these same gaps and barriers have vanished.

Today it is no longer necessary that we look to reason to build bridges between the ideal and the real, between mind and body, between spiritual and material. Since the universe is now seen as one and human consciousness is viewed as a whole, the possibility emerges for a truly holistic theology. John Macquarrie's criteria of consistency, coherence, and openness in the face of change apply to any and all future thinking about God, for one simply cannot isolate "religious truths" from any other realm of knowledge and experience.

By way of illustration, reflect for a few moments upon that passage from Genesis which has been so fundamental to the Judeo-Christian understanding of creation: "So God created man in his own image, in the image of God he created him; male and female he created them" (Gen. 1:27). Here the cardinal notion that God's very image is reflected in human nature is very clearly linked with the cardinal distinction between male and female. Yet the meaning of that distinction is one of the most hotly contested issues in science. It would be futile and self-defeating for a theologian to attempt *any* serious inquiry into the meaning of that biblical teaching without integrating the text with the latest scientific theories relating to human sexuality. As research proceeds rapidly along the whole frontier of science, in psychology and anthropology, in sociology and biology, and in history and chemistry, our awareness of what it means to exist as "male and female" is constantly changing and expanding. As we learn more and more about the factors shaping our existence in this peculiar arrangement between the sexes, we also learn a great deal that will impinge upon our understanding of what it means to exist as male and female in the image and likeness of God. Similarly, Paul's resounding affirmation to the Colossians, that Christ is "the image of the invisible God," the one in whom "all things hold together" (Col. 1:15, 17), remains little more than a pious and perhaps arrogant pronouncement unless and until the faith which makes such statements possible can be related to the science that has so much to say about how all things do in fact "hold together." It would be theologically suicidal to continue affirming the unity and interrelationship of all things in Christ without encompassing the wealth of scientific research pertaining to the actual relationships that connect all things. If God really is what the Judeo-Christian tradition has always affirmed, namely, the Alpha and the Omega, the Beginning and the End of all things, then God must also be the Beginning and the End of science as well. To put it another way, if God is in any sense real, then any inquiry into what is most real and ultimate in this world must have some bearing upon our understanding of the reality which is God.

In the age of dualistic thinking it was commonly asserted that, while reason could lead us to the point of acknowledgment that God exists, only revelation could lead to any knowledge of God's true nature. While we might rely upon logic to lead us toward the fact of God's existence, only religious experiences could make clear God's identity and character. This is the same thinking that lies at the root of Kant's declaration, "I have therefore found it necessary to deny *knowledge,* in order to make room for *faith.*" In the two hundred years since Kant it has become increasingly apparent that knowledge and faith cannot be so clearly separated, for there is a residue of faith which remains even after the most rigorous attempt to purge away all emotional or subjective factors so as to arrive at something called "pure reason." There are also elements of reason which remain even in the realm of "pure emotion": music, poetry, personal relationships. In fact, the scientific theories of Marx, Darwin, Freud, and Einstein have revealed the futility of trying to separate scientific knowledge from its roots in the rich soil of the human spirit. As Freud demonstrated so clearly, we are constantly and continually influenced by subconscious factors that can never be subjected to the sovereignty of the conscious mind.

In this context the irrational elements that lie at the heart of science become all the more apparent. For by its own initiative and within its own reach reason cannot grasp what is most real. As Einstein and Torrance both recognized, the order of the universe is revealed to us as much through faith as through any process of rational analysis. Faith does not begin where logic ends; rather, faith is required from the very beginning to the very end of the arduous search for life's deepest secrets. As the work of science and theology proceed apace, there comes a point when one must make what is essentially a character judgment of the cosmos. In the very attempt to integrate various experimental data with experiential fact, one eventually begins to wonder whether the universe is hospitable or alien to life. Either one sees the highest aspirations of our species as being rooted and grounded in reality or one concludes that our deepest aspirations are illusory.

It is the central affirmation of the Judeo-Christian faith that this cosmos is the creation of a just and loving God. There is a fundamental compatibility between the creation and the Creator. Though it is not easy to reconcile all the contradictory circumstances that we observe with this symbol of an all-loving God, still it is possible, reasonable, and profoundly desirable that we do so. For, if we do not see this cosmos to be a place which opens itself to our adoration, then it is unlikely that we will continue in the struggle to be the faithful stewards of the world.

Does the creation contain within it convincing evidence of a creator? Does the universe offer reliable clues pertaining to the reality of a just and loving God? To make such judgments one must draw upon the widest, broadest, and deepest sources of information. To ignore the findings of science is theologically irresponsible, and to ignore the deepest impulses of the human spirit is scientifically suicidal. To understand the universe we must understand it, in so far as it is possible, in its totality.

Scientific atheism consistently makes the mistake of trying to reduce the cosmos to its smallest, discrete components, whereas the religious or theological enterprise is to discern the cosmos as the sum of its varied parts. There is a strong consensus within the community of science, as well as within the community of faith, that the whole is greater, even far greater, than the sum of all its parts. Therefore, models of the universe which reduce reality to a mechanical process or an abstraction of the mind are defeated by the principle of consistency as well as by the principle of coherence.

The symbol of a personal God allows for the same crosscurrents of order and spontaneity, predictability and chance, regularity and novelty that science sees in nature. In this sense all the old arguments, which move from reason, order, and design in nature, must be combined with a complementary appeal to spontaneity, unpredictability, and mystery. When this is done and when the arguments are seen as finding a focal point in the symbol of the just and loving God, then it becomes clear that the Judeo-Christian tradition is not undermined by science; rather, it is confirmed as the most comprehensive, coherent, and compelling view available within western culture. In fact, from this perspective it can be seen that both agnostic humanism and atheistic science are essentially truncated versions of the Judeo-Christian faith.

Moreover, belief in a just and loving God is a stance that can be tested in the same way that scientific theories can. There are particular events and experiences that count for or against this faith. For example, the very existence of a scientific, technological culture is perhaps the most powerful confirmation of this faith, for it is the hope of this religion that civilization can be made compatible with the deepest aspirations of the human spirit. We can, with the aid of science and technology and with the guidance of religion, move this society toward closer realization of the justice and love of God. To the extent that we carry that faith into practice, we together offer up to God and to our fellow creatures the proof of our convictions. Yet, if we, on the contrary, fail to give our faith concrete expression in our personal and public lives, then this faith fails to find the proof it needs. In fact, a nuclear war which rendered this planet uninhabitable would be a precise refutation of the Judeo-Christian faith. For, while it still might be true in theory that the reality of a just and loving God could be verified on some other planet in some distant solar system, still, as far as we are aware, this planet is the decisive arena in which the truth or falsehood of the Judeo-Christian faith is to be decided. In the final analysis any proof for the existence of God must turn upon the hinge of the future. The final verdict is contingent upon our collective decisions in applying both the vast technologies made possible through science and the deep insights that arise from the soil of faith. If we can coordinate the very best that we have received in our faith with the very best we have achieved in our science, then we will have provided the world with an incontrovertible new proof for the reality of God. Still, in this nuclear age the final proof of our faith awaits our faithful transformation of hope into practice.

Short of a nuclear holocaust which renders our planet uninhabitable or radical improvements which transform human life within a short span of time, the best we have is an interim argument for God. In the corporate life of the church there is an opportunity to live out on a small scale what we see writ large as the destiny for a planet. To the extent that the love and justice of God can be realized in a community of faith, that community itself becomes the living proof of the reality to which it speaks and to which it prays. When, to the contrary, a given community of faith falls short of its faith, that faith is thoroughly defeated.

In the old world of dualistic thought it was believed that in science and in religion truth claims could be tested by a process of rational analysis. The laws of nature existed independently of the scientists who formulated them, and the laws of God existed separately and apart from the individuals who proclaimed them. Such is not the case today. We now know that knowledge emerges organically from the circumstances in which we live and move and have our being. Accordingly all faith statements must be studied and tested in the specific context in which they were made. Moreover, there cannot be a single, all-purpose argument for God. There is not and cannot be a simple statement of truth that works for all people in all times. A people struggling against oppressive institutions in the Third World will see God in very different ways than does a people who enjoys the benefits of a highly industrialized consumer society. Children reared by abusive parents will have a very different perspective in their faith than children who have been reared in the relative safety of a loving family. Each of us will arrive at a view of God which is consistent with the immediate circumstances in which we live, with the religious traditions into which we were born and reared (or the lack thereof), and with experiences of the world which change from day to day. No theologian can construct a system that will work for all people at all times. What theologians can and should do is to dispel those false, debilitating distinctions between religion and science, between religion and every other realm of human experience. In order that God may be experienced as the Alpha and the Omega, the Beginning and the End, the imagination must be freed from those narrow categories which carve reality itself into separate and distinct pieces. Theology can and should cooperate with science in its work of exploring the interconnective tissue of human consciousness itself and the interrelating structures of the world, so that it becomes possible once again to see God as the One in whom all things cohere. In this book I have drawn upon certain traditions in theology and certain trends in science to prepare the foundations for a new case for theism. From this point forward it is the reader's responsibility to construct an argument for God which is spun out of the varied circumstances of his or her own life.

While my own experience cannot be held up as normative for all readers, it may be pertinent to share one parable from my own life story. While writing this book I was also engaged in the process of building the little cabin in which it was written. In the process of constructing this small house I found it necessary to learn a variety of skills: the rudiments of architecture and design, of carpentry and cabinetmaking, of plumbing and electricity. Finally there was the moment of standing for the first time within the completed shell of this structure and enjoying the sense of shelter which it provides. To be sure, I felt, the whole *is* greater than the sum of all its parts. As Carl Jung found in the construction of his retreat home in Switzerland, he was actually making "a confession of faith in stone."[27] When one successfully coordinates all the elements of design and construction, the dwelling takes shape in such a way that it invites and welcomes its inhabitants, and the house becomes a home.

A successful house design provides not only for shelter from the world but also for a view of the world. A house has windows not only for letting light in but also for letting the inhabitants look out. The same is true of any successful theology. As the world is one, any future theological system must bring into a unifying vision all the varied elements of human experience. It must provide a theoretical framework in which to work out the problems of identity or salvation. Yet it must also provide a view of the world. The strongest possible argument for God is one which succeeds in providing a sense of personal identity together with a unifying vision of the whole.

Clearly, there is no argument for God which can take flight on the wings of logic alone. As we have seen, the very attempt to construct such a proof would be a contradiction in terms, and it would fly in the face of all we have learned in the past two hundred years of science. However, just as clearly, it is a matter of folly to anchor faith in the realm of disembodied spirituality or to found it upon the authority of religion alone. For such a faith tries to stand upon a rock which itself is a mere figment of the imagination. What we can and should do is demonstrate that belief in God is compatible with the highest and deepest aspirations of the human heart as well as with the broadest and widest discoveries of science. When it is shown that faith is internally consistent, coherent, and responsive to new insights which arise at the forward frontier of knowledge, then one has in fact established a new proof for God. The fact that all arguments for God must be continually revised and reformed does not defeat the undertaking. The fact that God cannot be pinned down with a certainty that is for once and forever, for one and all, does not count against the validity of a given proof. Nor should the failure of the traditional proofs lead toward the abandonment of the very effort to state the case for God in the strongest possible terms.

Modern theologians have surrendered to scientific atheism just at the moment this opponent was about to self-destruct. In the new age of God, as science and theology enter into new forms of partnership and as we see transformation and convergence taking place all along the horizons of consciousness, it is time to regain the confidence and creativity expressed in the old proofs for God. For, while nothing in this world can be pinned down with total certitude, we can come as close to proving God as we can to anything else that matters. Therefore let every thoughtful believer proceed with renewed confidence and creativity in the construction of a still more compelling case for the reality of God.

Notes

Introduction

1. Dietrich Bonhoeffer, *Letters and Papers from Prison,* revised and enlarged edition (New York: Macmillan, 1972), p. 178.

Chapter 1

1. Abraham Pais, *'Subtle is the Lord . . . ': The Science and the Life of Albert Einstein* (New York: Oxford University, 1982), p. 37.
2. Citation appears in "Celebrating Einstein" by William Stockton, *The New York Times Magazine* (Feb. 18, 1979), p. 50.
3. Werner Heisenberg, *Physics and Beyond: Encounters and Conversations* (New York: Harper and Row, 1971), p. 82.
4. Ibid., p. 85.
5. Ibid., p. 87.
6. Title of source unknown.
7. Fritjof Capra, *The Tao of Physics: An Exploration of the Parallels Between Modern Physics and Eastern Mysticism* (New York: Bantam, 1977), p. 56.

Chapter 2

1. Sigmund Freud, *The Future of an Illusion,* revised edition (New York: Norton, 1961), pp. 15–16.
2. Ibid., p. 17.
3. Ibid., p. 17.
4. Sigmund Freud, *Civilization and Its Discontents* (New York: Norton, 1961), p. 21.
5. *The Future of an Illusion,* p. 21.
6. As cited in Walter Kaufmann, *Critique of Religion and Philosophy* (Garden City, NY: Doubleday, 1961), p. 417
7. Sigmund Freud, *New Introductory Lectures on Psychoanalysis* (New York: Norton, 1964), p. 167.
8. *The Future of an Illusion,* p. 15.
9. Sigmund Freud, *Beyond the Pleasure Principle* (New York: Bantam, 1959), pp. 101–2.
10. Ibid., p. 89.
11. *Civilization and Its Discontents,* p. 69.

Chapter 3

1. Neal C. Gillespie, *Charles Darwin and the Problem of Creation* (Chicago: University of Chicago, 1979), p. 87.
2. Gertrude Himmelfarb, *Darwin and the Darwinian Revolution* (Garden City, NY: Doubleday, 1959), p. 65.
3. Ibid., p. 75.
4. Ibid., p. 75.
5. Ibid., p. 79.
6. Ibid., p. 79.
7. Ibid., p. 80.
8. Charles Darwin, *The Autobiography of Charles Darwin*, ed. Nora Barlow (London: Collins, 1958), pp. 85–87.
9. Charles Darwin, *The Origin of Species* (New York: Collier and Son, 1909), p. 500.
10. Charles Darwin, *The Descent of Man; and Selection in Relation to Sex* (New York: A. L. Burt, 1874), p. 694.
11. William Paley, *Natural Theology: or, Evidences of the Existence and Attributes of the Deity, Collected from the Appearances of Nature* (Boston: Gould, Kendall and Lincoln, 1849), p. 6.
12. Ibid., p. 6.
13. Ibid., p. 13.
14. Ibid., p. 26.
15. Ibid., p. 26.
16. Ibid., pp. 293–94.
17. Darwin, *The Autobiography of Charles Darwin*, p. 87.
18. Gillespie, *Charles Darwin and the Problem of Creation*, p. 83.
19. Ibid., p. 133.
20. Ibid., p. 84.
21. Stephen Jay Gould, *The Panda's Thumb: More Reflections in Natural History* (New York: Norton, 1982), p. 64.
22. Ibid., p. 66.
23. Darwin, *The Origin of Species*, p. 487.
24. Ibid., p. 91.
25. Ibid., p. 506.
26. Ibid., pp. 88–89.
27. Ibid., pp. 505–6.
28. Quoted in Gillespie, *Charles Darwin and the Problem of Creation*, p. 128.
29. Darwin, *The Origin of Species*, p. 506.
30. Gillespie, *Charles Darwin and the Problem of Creation*, p. 87.
31. Ibid., p. 87.
32. Gould, *The Panda's Thumb*, pp. 20–21.
33. Ibid., p. 26.
34. Ibid., p. 20.
35. Ibid., p. 139.

Chapter 4

1. Karl Marx and Friedrich Engels, *The Communist Manifesto* (New York: Penguin, 1967), pp. 120–21.
2. Saul K. Padover, *Karl Marx: An Intimate Biography* (New York: New American Library, 1980), p. 6.
3. Ibid., p. 9.
4. Ibid., pp. 54–55.
5. Thomas W. Ogletree (ed.), *Openings for Marxist-Christian Dialogue* (Nashville: Abingdon, 1968), p. 75.
6. James Bentley, *Between Marx and Christ: The Dialogue in German Speaking Europe, 1870–1970* (London: Verso Editions, 1982), p. 99.
7. Robert C. Tucker (ed.), *The Marx-Engels Reader* (New York: Norton, 1972), pp. 11–12.
8. Ibid., p. 603.
9. Eugene Kamenka (ed.), *The Portable Karl Marx* (New York: Viking, 1983), p. 462.
10. Ibid., pp. 444–45.
11. Ibid., p. 447.
12. Ibid., p. 162.
13. Ibid., p. 177.
14. Marx and Engels, *The Communist Manifesto*, p. 95.
15. Ibid., p. 95.
16. James H. Billington, *Fire in the Minds of Men: Origins of the Revolutionary Faith* (New York: Basic, 1980), p. 275.
17. Kamenka, *The Portable Karl Marx*, p. 94.
18. Bentley, *Between Marx and Christ*, pp. 67–68, quoting Karl Barth, *Church Dogmatics*, Volume III Part 2, *The Doctrine of Creation* (Edinburgh: T. & T. Clark, 1960), pp. 389–90.
19. Bentley, *Between Marx and Christ*, p. 68.

Chapter 5

1. Pierre Teilhard de Chardin, *The Divine Milieu: An Essay on the Interior Life* (New York: Harper and Row, 1968), p. 112.
2. Ibid., p. 46.
3. Pierre Teilhard de Chardin, *Christianity and Evolution* (New York: Harcourt Brace Jovanovich, 1971), p. 99.
4. Ibid., pp. 127, 130.
5. *The Divine Milieu*, p. 18.
6. Ibid., p. 17.
7. Ibid., p. 13.
8. Mary and Ellen Lukas, *Teilhard* (Garden City, NY: Doubleday, 1977), pp. 31–32.
9. Stephen Jay Gould, *Hen's Teeth and Horse's Toes* (New York: Norton, 1983), p. 225.

10. *Christianity and Evolution,* p. 130.
11. Pierre Teilhard de Chardin, *Human Energy* (New York: Harcourt Brace Jovanovich, 1971), p. 163.
12. Ibid., pp. 168–69.
13. Ibid., p. 171.
14. Ibid., p. 172.
15. Ibid., p. 174.
16. Gould, *Hen's Teeth and Horse's Toes,* p. 250.
17. Pierre Teilhard de Chardin, *The Phenomenon of Man* (New York: Harper and Row, 1961), pp. 141–42.
18. Ibid., p. 220.
19. Ibid., p. 283.
20. Ibid., p. 224.
21. Ibid., p. 250.
22. Ibid., pp. 284–85.
23. *Christianity and Evolution,* p. 194.
24. Ibid., p. 240.
25. Figure adapted from diagram appearing in Pierre Teilhard de Chardin's *The Future of Man* (New York: Harper and Row, 1969), p. 269.
26. *Human Energy,* p. 180.
27. Ibid., p. 181.

Chapter 6

1. Hannah Tillich, *From Time to Time* (New York: Stein and Day, 1973), p. 241.
2. Ibid., p. 242.
3. Wilhelm and Marion Pauck, *Paul Tillich: His Life and Thought.* Volume 1: *Life* (New York: Harper and Row, 1976), p. 1.
4. Ibid., p. 5.
5. Ibid., p. 8.
6. Paul Tillich, *On the Boundary: An Autobiographical Sketch* (New York: Scribner's, 1966), p. 18.
7. Ibid., p. 16.
8. Hannah Tillich, *From Time to Time,* p. 242.
9. Pauck, *Paul Tillich,* p. 37.
10. Paul Tillich, *Systematic Theology,* volume 1 (Chicago: University of Chicago, 1951), p. 7.
11. Pauck, *Paul Tillich,* pp. 40–41.
12. Ibid., p. 51.
13. Ibid., p. 92.
14. Paul Tillich, *Theology of Culture* (New York: Oxford University, 1959), p. 3.
15. Ibid., pp. 4–5.
16. *Systematic Theology,* volume 1, p. 18.

17. Ibid., pp. 18–19.
18. Paul Tillich, *The Religious Situation* (New York: Meridian, 1956), p. 62.
19. *Systematic Theology*, volume 1, p. 212.
20. Paul Tillich, *Biblical Religion and the Search for Ultimate Reality* (Chicago: University of Chicago, 1955), p. 13.
21. *On the Boundary*, p. 88.
22. Paul Tillich, *The Socialist Decision* (New York: Harper and Row, 1977), p. 81.
23. Ibid., p. xiii.
24. *The Religious Situation*, p. 107.
25. Ibid., p. 107.
26. *Systematic Theology*, volume 1, p. 206.
27. Ibid., p. 205.
28. Ibid., p. 205, emphasis mine.
29. Ibid., p. 15.
30. *Theology of Culture*, p. 42.
31. Paul Tillich, *Systematic Theology*, volume 3 (Chicago: University of Chicago, 1963), pp. 15–30.
32. Ibid., p. 15.
33. *Theology of Culture*, p. 130.
34. Ibid., p. 130.
35. Ibid., p. 130.
36. Ibid., p. 130.
37. Ibid., pp. 130–31.
38. Ibid., p. 131.
39. Ibid., pp. 131–32.

Chapter 7

1. Gary Zukav, *The Dancing Wu Li Masters: An Overview of the New Physics* (New York: Bantam, 1980), p. 72.
2. Fritjof Capra, *The Tao of Physics: An Exploration of the Parallels Between Modern Physics and Eastern Mysticism* (New York: Bantam, 1977), pp. 4–5.
3. Ibid., pp. 8–9.
4. Zukav, *The Dancing Wu Li Masters*, pp. 29–30.
5. Ibid., p. 31.
6. Capra, *The Tao of Physics*, p. 11.
7. Ibid., p. 117.
8. Zukav, *The Dancing Wu Li Masters*, p. 107.
9. Ibid., p. 91.
10. Capra, *The Tao of Physics*, p. 180.
11. Zukav, *The Dancing Wu Li Masters*, p. 193.
12. Ibid., p. 217.
13. Ibid., p. 205.

14. Ibid., pp. 154–55.
15. Ibid., p. 88.
16. Capra, *The Tao of Physics*, p. 11.
17. Zukav, *The Dancing Wu Li Masters*, p. 114.
18. Ibid., p. 281.
19. Capra, *The Tao of Physics*, pp. 276–77.
20. Ibid., p. 279.

Chapter 8

1. Tillich, *Systematic Theology*, volume 1, pp. 204–5.
2. Søren Kierkegaard, *The Concept of Dread* (Princeton, NJ: Princeton University, 1957), p. 125.
3. Citation in Antony Flew, *God and Philosophy* (New York: Harcourt, Brace and World, 1966), p. 12.
4. Hans Küng, *Does God Exist?: An Answer for Today* (Garden City, NY: Doubleday, 1980), p. 534.
5. Ibid., p. 534.
6. Tillich, *Systematic Theology*, volume 1, p. 205.
7. Ibid., p. 206.
8. Ibid., p. 208.
9. Ibid., p. 210.
10. Küng, *Does God Exist?*, p. 535.
11. Ibid., p. 535.
12. Ibid., p. 534.
13. Ibid., p. 540.
14. Ibid., p. 540.
15. Ibid., pp. 570–71.
16. John Macquarrie, *Principles of Christian Theology*, second edition (New York: Scribner's, 1977), p. 49.
17. Ibid., p. 56.
18. Ibid., pp. 147–48.
19. Thomas F. Torrance, *Transformation and Convergence in the Frame of Knowledge: Explorations in the Interrelations of Scientific and Theological Enterprise* (Grand Rapids: Eerdmans, 1984), p. 78.
20. Cited in Pais, *'Subtle is the Lord . . . '*, p. 27.
21. Thomas F. Torrance, *Transformation and Convergence*, p. 251.
22. Cited by Torrance, ibid., p. 253.
23. Ibid., p. 254.
24. Ibid., p. 256.
25. Ibid., p. 257.
26. Bonhoeffer, *Letters and Papers from Prison*, p. 178.
27. Carl Jung, *Memories, Dreams, Reflections*, recorded and edited by Aniela Jaffé (New York: Random House, 1963), p. 223.

Bibliography

Adams, James Luther. *Paul Tillich's Philosophy of Culture, Science and Religion.* New York: Harper and Row, 1965.

Barbour, Ian G. *Issues in Science and Religion.* New York: Harper and Row, 1971.

Barnett, Lincoln. *The Universe and Dr. Einstein.* New York: Harper and Brothers, 1948.

Bentley, James. *Between Marx and Christ: The Dialogue in German Speaking Europe, 1870–1970.* London: Verso Editions, 1982.

Bettelheim, Bruno. *Freud and Man's Soul.* New York: Vintage Books, 1984.

Billington, James H. *Fire in the Minds of Men: Origins of the Revolutionary Faith.* New York: Basic Books, 1980.

Boder, M. M. *Karl Marx's Interpretation of History.* New York: W. W. Norton, 1965.

Bondi, Hermann. *Relativity and Common Sense: A New Approach to Einstein.* Garden City, NY: Doubleday, 1964.

Bonhoeffer, Dietrich. *Letters and Papers from Prison.* Revised and enlarged edition. New York: Macmillan, 1972.

Born, Max. *My Life and Views.* New York: Scribner's, 1968.

Bronowski, J. *Science and Human Values.* New York: Harper and Row, 1965.

Bultmann, Rudolf. *Jesus Christ and Mythology.* New York: Scribner's, 1958.

Capra, Fritjof. *The Tao of Physics: An Exploration of the Parallels Between Modern Physics and Eastern Mysticism.* New York: Bantam Books, 1977.

Darwin, Charles. *The Autobiography of Charles Darwin,* ed. Nora Barlow. London: Collins, 1958.

———. *The Descent of Man; and Selection in Relation to Sex.* New York: A. L. Burt, 1874.

———. *The Origin of Species.* New York: P. F. Collier and Son, 1909.

Dawkins, Richard. *The Selfish Gene.* Oxford: Oxford University Press, 1976.

Farrington, Benjamin. *What Darwin Really Said.* New York: Schocken Books, 1982.

Flew, Antony. *God and Philosophy.* New York: Harcourt, Brace and World, 1966.

Freud, Sigmund. *Beyond the Pleasure Principle*. London: Hogarth Press, 1950.

———. *Civilization and Its Discontents*. New York: W. W. Norton, 1961.

———. *The Ego and the Id*. New York: W. W. Norton, 1962.

———. *The Future of an Illusion*. Revised edition. New York: W. W. Norton, 1961.

———. *A General Introduction to Psychoanalysis*. New York: Washington Square Press, 1952.

———. *Moses and Monotheism*. New York: Vintage Books, 1939.

———. *New Introductory Lectures on Psychoanalysis*. New York: W. W. Norton, 1964.

———. *Sexuality and the Psychology of Love*. New York: Macmillan, 1963.

———. *Totem and Taboo*. New York: Vintage Books, 1946.

Gilkey, Langdon. *Society and the Sacred*. New York: Crossroad, 1981.

Gillespie, Neal C. *Charles Darwin and the Problem of Creation*. Chicago: University of Chicago Press, 1979.

Gould, Stephen Jay. *The Panda's Thumb: More Reflections in Natural History*. New York: W. W. Norton, 1982.

———. *Hen's Teeth and Horse's Toes*. New York: W. W. Norton, 1983.

Hall, Calvin S. *A Primer of Freudian Psychology*. New York: World Publishing Co., 1954.

Heimann, Eduard. *Reason and Faith in Modern Society*. Middletown, CT: Wesleyan University Press, 1961.

Heisenberg, Werner. *Physics and Beyond: Encounters and Conversations*. New York: Harper and Row, 1971.

Himmelfarb, Gertrude. *Darwin and the Darwinian Revolution*. Garden City, NY: Doubleday, 1959.

Jung, Carl. *Memories, Dreams, Reflections*. Recorded and edited by Aniela Jaffé. New York: Random House, 1963.

Kamenka, Eugene (ed.). *The Portable Karl Marx*. New York: Viking Press, 1983.

Kaufmann, Walter. *Critique of Religion and Philosophy*. Garden City, NY: Doubleday, 1961.

Kierkegaard, Søren. *The Concept of Dread*. Princeton: Princeton University Press, 1957.

King, Thomas M. and James F. Salmon. *Teilhard and the Unity of Knowledge*. New York: Paulist Press, 1983.

Küng, Hans. *Does God Exist?: An Answer for Today*. Garden City, NY: Doubleday, 1980.

Leakey, Richard E. and Roger Lewin. *Origins. What New Discoveries Reveal about the Emergence of Our Species and Its Possible Future*. New York: E. P. Dutton, 1977.

Lukas, Mary and Ellen. *Teilhard*. Garden City, NY: Doubleday, 1977.

Macquarrie, John. *Principles of Christian Theology*. Second edition. New York: Scribner's, 1977.

——. *Thinking about God.* New York: Harper and Row, 1975.

Marcuse, Herbert. *Eros and Civilization: A Philosophical Inquiry into Freud.* New York: Vintage Books, 1961.

Marx, Karl and Friedrich Engels. *The Communist Manifesto.* New York: Penguin Books, 1967.

Nebelsick, Harold F. *Theology and Science in Mutual Modification.* New York: Oxford University Press, 1981.

Oestreicher, Paul (ed.). *The Christian Marxist Dialogue.* New York: Macmillan, 1969.

Ogletree, Thomas W. (ed.). *Openings for Marxist-Christian Dialogue.* Nashville: Abingdon, 1968.

Padover, Saul K. *Karl Marx: An Intimate Biography.* New York: New American Library, 1980.

Pais, Abraham. *'Subtle is the Lord . . . ': The Science and the Life of Albert Einstein.* New York: Oxford University Press, 1982.

Paley, William. *Natural Theology: or, Evidences of the Existence and Attributes of the Deity, Collected from the Appearances of Nature.* Boston: Gould, Kendall and Lincoln, 1849.

Pauck, Wilhelm and Marion. *Paul Tillich: His Life and Thought.* Volume 1: *Life.* New York: Harper and Row, 1976.

Ricoeur, Paul. *Freud and Philosophy: An Essay on Interpretation.* New Haven: Yale University Press, 1970.

Russell, Bertrand. *The ABC of Relativity.* New York: New American Library, 1959.

Soelle, Dorothee. *Political Theology.* Philadelphia: Fortress, 1974.

Stockton, William. "Celebrating Einstein." P. 50 in *The New York Times Magazine,* Feb. 18, 1979.

Teilhard de Chardin, Pierre. *Christianity and Evolution.* New York: Harcourt Brace Jovanovich, 1971.

——. *The Divine Milieu: An Essay on the Interior Life.* New York: Harper and Row, 1968.

——. *The Future of Man.* New York: Harper and Row, 1969.

——. *Human Energy.* New York: Harcourt Brace Jovanovich, 1971.

——. *Hymn of the Universe.* New York: Harper and Row, 1972.

——. *The Phenomenon of Man.* New York: Harper and Row, 1961.

Tillich, Hannah. *From Time to Time.* New York: Stein and Day, 1973.

Tillich, Paul. *Biblical Religion and the Search for Ultimate Reality.* Chicago: University of Chicago Press, 1955.

——. *The Courage to Be.* New Haven: Yale University Press, 1952.

——. *The Dynamics of Faith.* New York: Harper and Row, 1957.

——. *The Eternal Now.* New York: Scribner's, 1963.

——. *The New Being.* New York: Scribner's, 1955.

——. *On the Boundary: An Autobiographical Sketch.* New York: Scribner's, 1966.

——. *The Religious Situation.* New York: Meridian Books, 1956.

―――. *The Socialist Decision.* New York: Harper and Row, 1977.

―――. *Systematic Theology.* 3 volumes. Chicago: University of Chicago Press, 1951–1963.

―――. *Theology of Culture.* New York: Oxford University Press, 1959.

Torrance, Thomas F. *Transformation and Convergence in the Frame of Knowledge: Explorations in the Interrelations of Scientific and Theological Enterprise.* Grand Rapids: Eerdmans, 1984.

―――. *Divine and Contingent Order.* Oxford: Oxford University Press, 1981.

Tucker, Robert C. (ed.). *The Marx-Engels Reader.* New York: W. W. Norton, 1972.

Vidler, Alec R. *The Church in an Age of Revolution: 1789 to the Present Day.* New York: Penguin Books, 1961.

Whitehead, Alfred North. *Science and the Modern World.* New York: New American Library, 1948.

Zukav, Gary. *The Dancing Wu Li Masters: An Overview of the New Physics.* New York: Bantam Books, 1980.

Index